Connections

The RescueLogic Guide to Configuring Ports and Panels

RESCUE**LOGIC**®
"Safety Made Simple"

Cadgraphics Incorporated
Makers of RescueLogic Software for Fire and Security Systems

PO Box 11737
St. Paul, MN 55111-0737

Website: www.rescuelogic.com
Email: info@rescuelogic.com
Phone: (612) 722-3233

ISBN 978-0692253717

Table of Contents

Ports and Panels....1
Things You'll Need....1
Port and Panel Basics....2
A Typical Installation....2
Configure Panels for your Site....3
Create a List of Your Panels....3
Change the Panel ID....4
Add New Panels to the List....5
Delete Unused Panels....6
Panel Types....7
Pseudo Points....8
Modify the Values of Your Pseudo Points....9
Device State Mapping....9
Channel Applications....10
Using Channel Applications....10
Assign Channel Numbers....11
Script Panel Types....12
Define Patterns for Data Extraction....13
Test Your Scripts....14
Communication Paths....17
Configure Your Communication Paths....17
Edit Your COM Ports....18
Add a Reset Map....23
Serial Connections....24
COM Ports....24
COM Port to COM Port Connections....25
Ethernet Connections: Add a MOXA Device....26
Configure Operating Settings....29
Configure Serial Settings....30
Configure Network Settings....31
Questions or Comments?....32

Helpful Hint: This guide is illustrated with actual RescueLogic screen images, which were captured on a computer that runs Windows 7. If your computer uses a different Windows operating system, your RescueLogic windows might look different, but you will follow the same step-by-step procedures.

Ports and Panels

With RescueLogic, you can monitor a single alarm panel or an entire network of controls — even if your system is made up of panels and devices from more than one manufacturer. This guide will show you how to configure your RescueLogic system to recognize and receive data from the panels on your site.

You have two options: you can either connect your panels to an Ethernet network or you can hard-wire the panels directly to your computer with RS232 cables.

Things You'll Need

To connect alarm panels to your computer network, you will need:

- A list of all the panels you'd like to connect, including manufacturer and model numbers.

If you plan to connect your panels to an Ethernet network, you will need:

- A MOXA NPort 5110A serial device server.
- MOXA utility software. You'll get a software CD with each device. You can also download the software from the MOXA website at www.moxa.com.
- Network information. You'll need to get a static IP address from the network administrator wherever a serial server is to be installed. For each serial server, the network administrator should also provide values for the Subnet Mask, Default Gateway, and possibly DNS Servers. (See page 31 for more details.)
- The network administrator should also know that the serial servers will connect using, by default, TCP Port 4001. It can be changed. TCP Port 23 is a common alternate. (See page 29 for the screen with the TCP Port setting.)
- Serial Port information. The alarm panel manufacturer's documentation should show you the RS232 serial port settings. These include: baud rate; data bits, stop bits, and parity. See page 8 for the screen with serial settings to match up with the settings of your alarm panel. You will also need the wiring information for the RS232 (or EIA232) connection. Many alarm panels suggest a serial printer would be an optional accessory wired to this port.

You can also connect your panels to your computer ports with RS232 cables. In that case, you will need:

- An adaptor cable with a 9-pin connector at the computer end. The connection on the other end will need to fit your panel. Most often, you'll simply wire that end of the cable to a terminal strip.

In some cases, you will need to add a serial port to your alarm panel.

- If your panel doesn't have a built-in serial port, most manufacturers can offer optional modules that will work. Siemens, for example, offers a Remote Printer Module (RPM). For details, check the manual that came with your panel, consult the manufacturer, or call your fire alarm installer.

Port and Panel Basics

In order for RescueLogic to receive information about alarms and devices on your site, you will need to connect your alarm panels to your RescueLogic computer. While every panel formats data in its own way — depending on the manufacturer — most come equipped with a COM port that can be connected to a printer. With RescueLogic, you can also use that COM port to connect an alarm panel to a computer.

In fact, with RescueLogic you can actually monitor an entire network of control panels through a single COM port. You can hard wire your panels directly to your RescueLogic computer, or, if your RescueLogic computer is more than 50 feet from the panel, you can use your IP network, twisted pair copper wire, fiber optic cable, or a wireless transmitter to connect the two.

Alarm panels and your RescueLogic computer share a common language: ASCII data. RescueLogic translates that data into plain English, and displays it on color-coded lists, graphic images, and maps and floor plans.

RescueLogic also combines panel data in ways that make it more user-friendly. In most alarm systems, every device has a panel address number: 1001, 1002, or 1003, for example. If your facility has three alarm panels on site — three *nodes*, in other words — each node might assign those same three numbers to three separate devices. You could have several devices that are all assigned the same address, but different nodes. RescueLogic eliminates the confusion by combining node numbers and addresses, so each device is distinct.

A Typical Installation

Here is a prototypical installation that includes five alarm panels. One alarm panel is directly connected to a COM port. A second alarm panel is connected to the main computer with RS485 converters, to extend the connection range. A third alarm panel uses RS232/EIA232 cable connect to a TCP/IP converter, to exchange data over the building's local area network. A two-node network of alarm panels also connects to the LAN via TCP/IP protocol.

Of course, Ethernet allows you to extend your RescueLogic system to monitor panels over the Internet. A serial server at each panel will transmit every event in real time.

This illustration also shows how RescueLogic can use hyperlinks to connect a closed-circuit video camera and HVAC building controls.

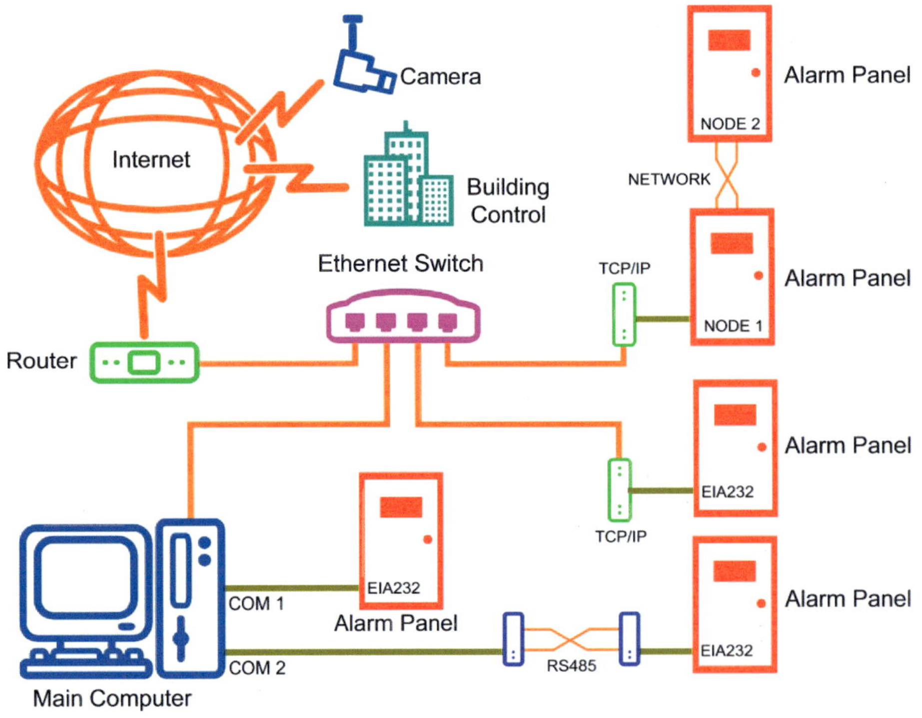

Configure Panels for your Site

The RescueLogic database contains information about the types of panels on your site. You can specify information about each panel in your system. If, for example, your facility has three panels — all of the same make and model — you will create three system panels with one panel type.

Open Configuration Manager. Go to the "Setup" drop-down menu and click on "System Panels."

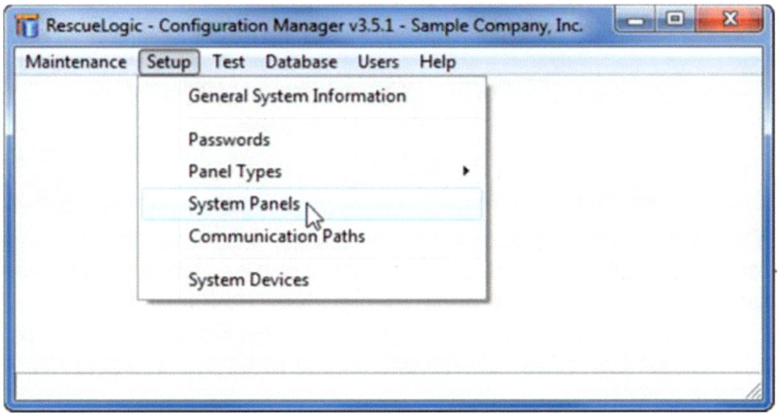

Create a List of Your Panels

The "System Panel Maintenance" window will open. You will see two default panel examples, named "Fire" and "Security." The example setup has two Silent Knight alarm panels — one dedicated to fire alarm functions, and another panel dedicated to security functions. In this example, we will look at the fire alarm panel. Choose the first one, labeled "Fire" from the drop-down list. Then click "Select."

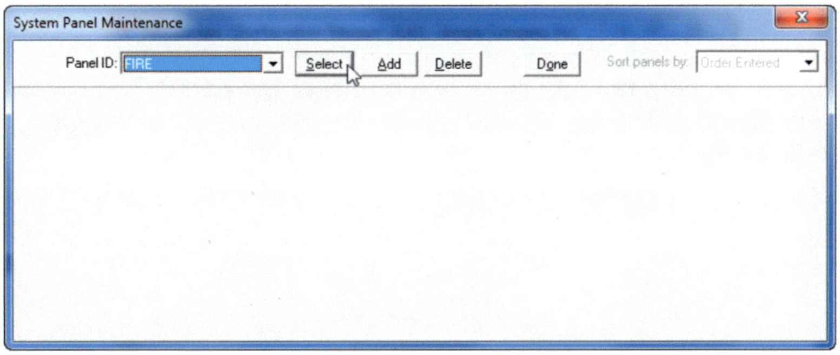

The Panel ID is labeled FIRE to distinguish it from our other example panel used for security alarms.

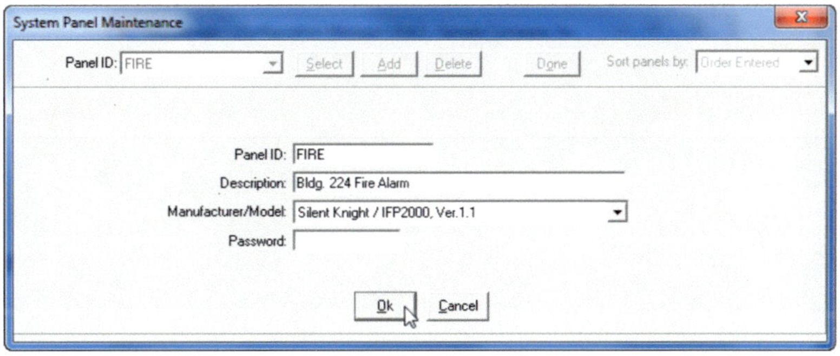

Change the Panel ID

Click in the Panel ID field, and change the text to "NODE 1."

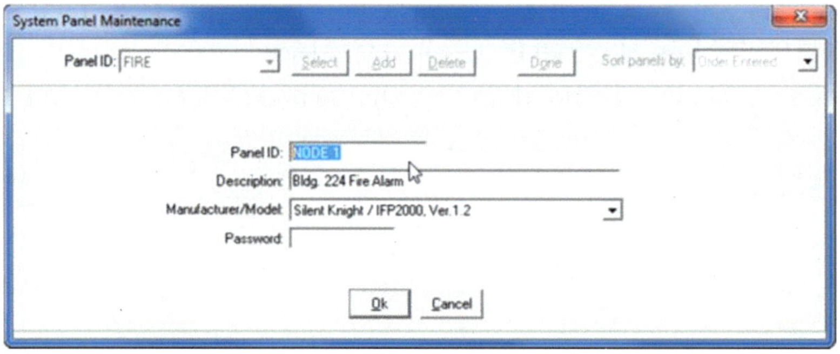

This works regardless of if the two panels are connected together or not. Each is an independent node, or data gathering point. You may be more familiar with network names, such as "Node 1." The next field, Description, allows you to enter a longer, expanded label in addition to each ID. The information you enter will be displayed on the System Watch screen, so it should make sense to your end users. Be specific, and use a name that everyone on your staff will recognize: "Sample Company Headquarters," for example, as opposed to a more generic "Panel A." When you are through, click "OK."

Helpful Hint: The Panel ID does not have to match the messages that the control panel sends. The Panel ID you enter on this screen will simply be displayed to System Watch users. If you have two networks of panels connected to one RescueLogic computer, for example, the first network might connect three panels: "Node 1," "Node 2," and "Node 3." You might want to differentiate the panels on the second network by adding a prefix number "Node 2-1," "Node 2-2," and "Node 2-3." Then, go back and ID the first network as "Node 1-1," "Node 1-2," and "Node 1-3."

Click on the drop-down arrow to see the manufacturer and model of the panel. The sample database uses Silent Knight as an example; if your site includes panels from other manufacturers, each type is added to the database, and will appear in the drop-down list.

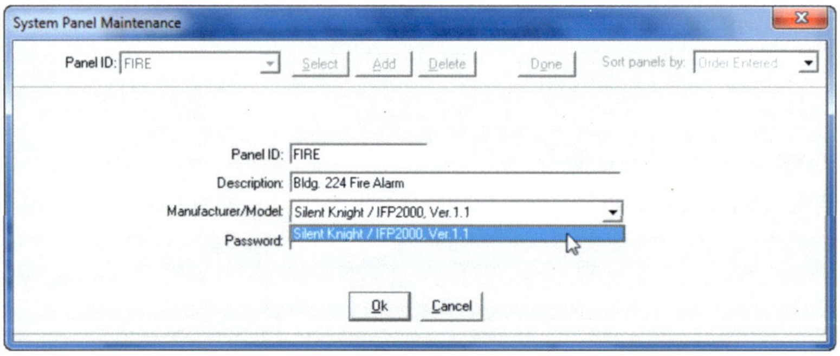

Helpful Hint: If this is the first time you've seen the System Panel list, don't be too concerned about the exact text. Just make each panel different from one another. At any time, and you can come back and change the labels after you've seen how they look in System Watch.

Add New Panels to the List

To add a new system panel to the pre-set list, click "Add."

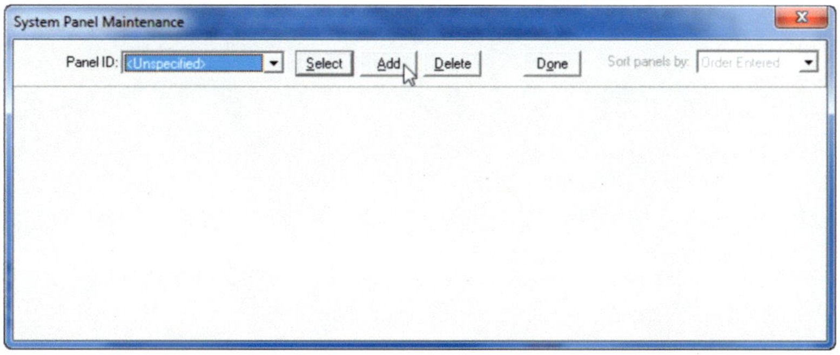

You will see the same fields to customize for your added panel. Simply replace the bracketed text with the names you used to overwrite the existing default panels. If you have more than one manufacturer/model, choose the correct one from the drop-down list.

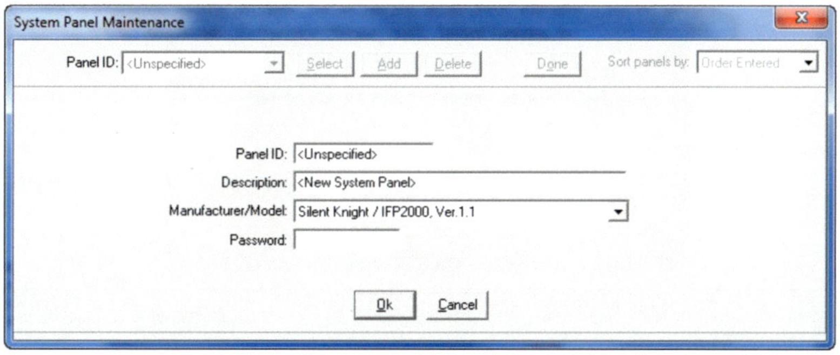

Give your new panel an ID, such as "Node 2," and a clear description that everyone on your staff will recognize. Select the correct manufacturer and model, and then click "OK." After the last new panel type has been added to the system, click "Done."

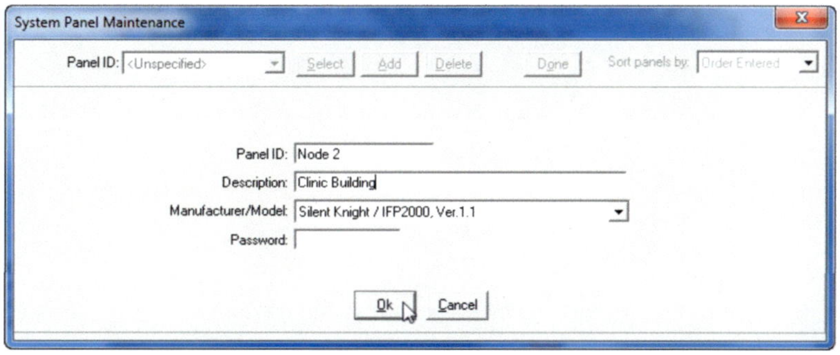

Helpful Hint: RescueLogic is programmed to work with a wide range of panels. RescueLogic also offers a Software Developers Kit that makes it possible to develop additional drivers to work with any panel. Email info@rescuelogic.com for details.

Delete Unused Panels

If you have only one system panel on your site, delete the extra one — either fire or security — from our sample database.

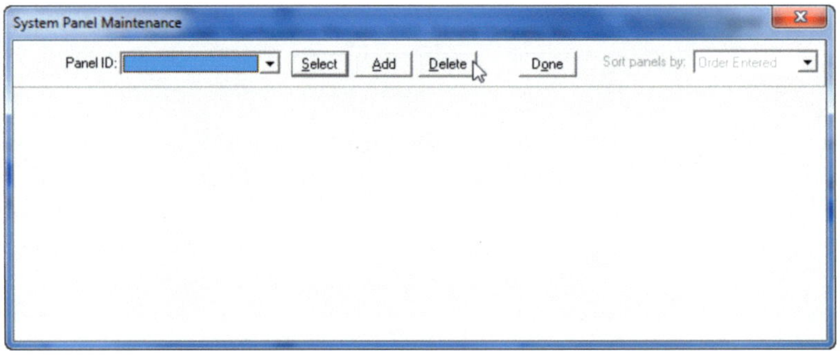

You will be asked to confirm the deletion. Click "Yes" to delete.

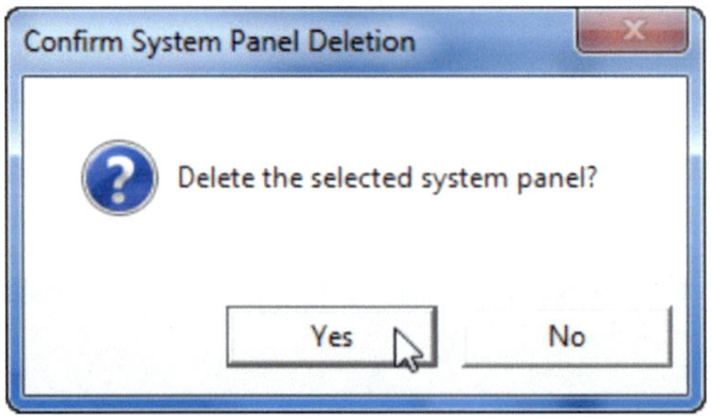

Helpful Hint: If you delete a system panel, you will wipe out RescueLogic's link with any devices that were associated with that panel. The devices themselves will remain in the database until you manually associate their addresses with a panel or delete them. However, you should only delete a panel if you also intend to delete the associated devices — as when you remove a sample panel from the default database, or if you are installing a new replacement panel with a new series of device addresses.

You can modify, add, or remove panels at any time. You don't need to set up your entire system all at once.

Panel Types

RescueLogic uses three methods of interfacing panels: Legacy Panels, Channel Applications, and Script Panel Types. First, we'll show you how to define Legacy Panel Types.

To define the panels on your site, open Configuration Manager, choose the Setup Menu, mouse over Panel Types, and then choose Legacy Panel Types.

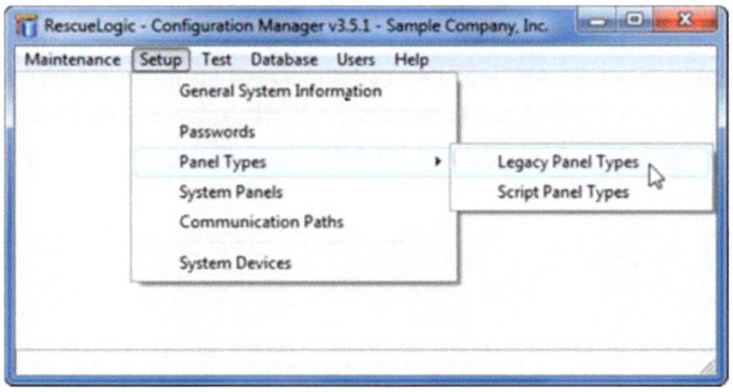

Use the drop-down menu to view a list of pre-set panel types. If your panel is not listed, click "Add." Enter a name and model number for your panel type. The name and model you type in are not fields that need to match anything specific; they are strictly for your own reference.

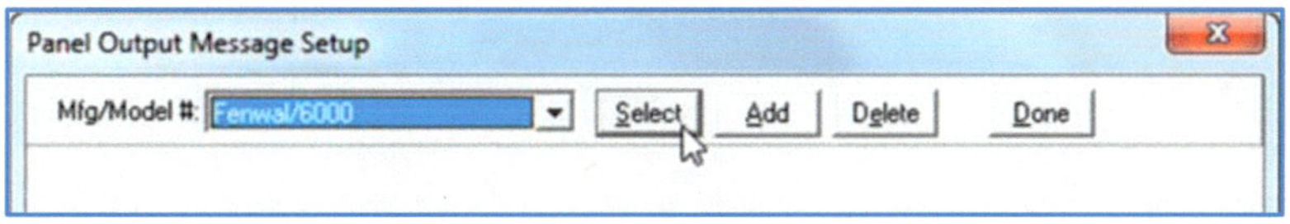

You will see a form to enter values that determine how messages from the particular type of control panel are to be interpreted. The purpose of these variables is to allow behavior of your system to vary from other systems, and also adapt to firmware changes of the control panel in the future.

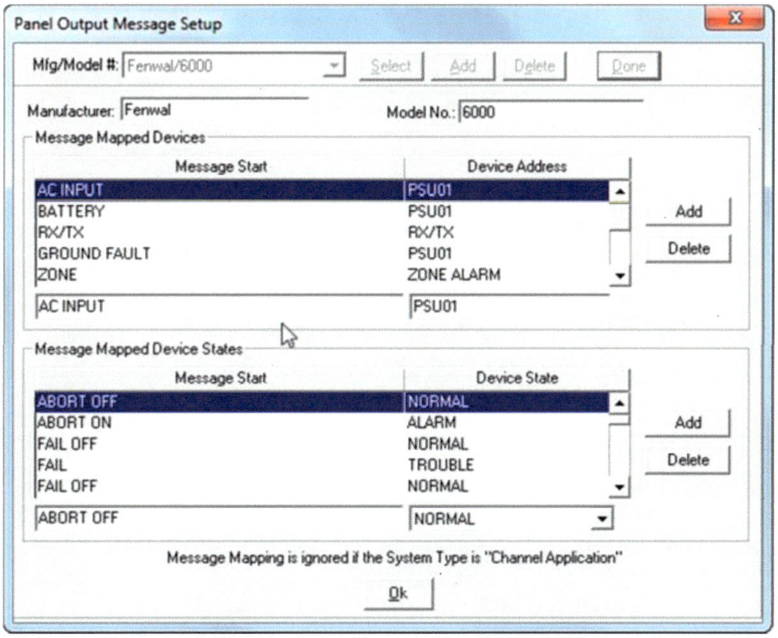

Pseudo Points

Some control panels have unique messages, such as low-battery warnings, that don't follow the normal device-address format. If you want to include them in your RescueLogic system, you will need to create an address, or *pseudo point*, that can be assigned to each message that you want to identify as a device. Then you will be able to locate those devices on a background map or floor plan.

The top half of the Panel Output Message form allows you to map messages to pseudo points. In this example, a message starting with AC INPUT is mapped to an address of PS01. Note that the next line item and also the third line item are also mapped to the same address, PS01. That is because, in this system, all three of those messages apply to the power supply, and the end user only wants one point to be created for any of those messages. The result will be that PS01 will appear in the Address field on the System Watch list, and underneath the icon on the floor plan.

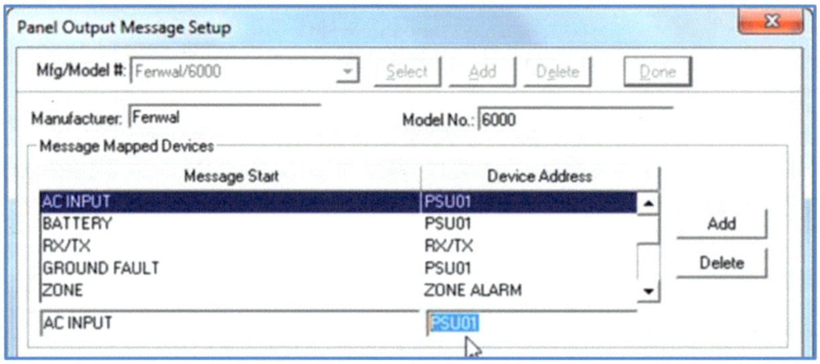

Alternately, you could assign three separate addresses to those three messages. In the next example, the same three messages are assigned to unique addresses, which will create three independent devices in the database. That way, if two or more events occur simultaneously, you'll see separate messages about each one. Then, as conditions are restored to normal, the state of each device will be reflected independently.

Here you see that AC INPUT has an address of 120 VAC, the address for BATTERY is BATTERY, and GROUND FAULT is GROUND.

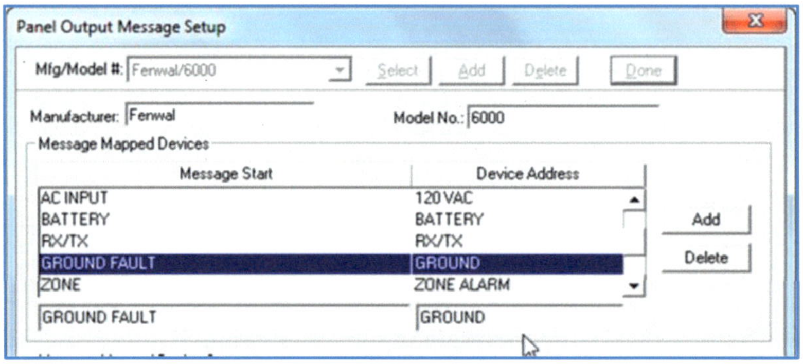

Helpful Hint: To test your address assignments, run System Monitor and make the panel report the message by activating the event. For example, if you have mapped the phrase "BATTERY FAILURE" to a new address called "BATTERY," try disconnecting the battery while System Monitor is running. A new pseudo device with the address "BATTERY" will be automatically added to the database, and it should appear in the System Watch list as a trouble. When you replace the wire, and the panel detects the batteries again, it will restore to normal, and its color will be green.

Modify the Values of Your Pseudo Points

Modify an item in the list by clicking on it to see the values in the edit boxes below. Simply click on the <Message Start> and <Device Address> lines to highlight them, and type in your new text.

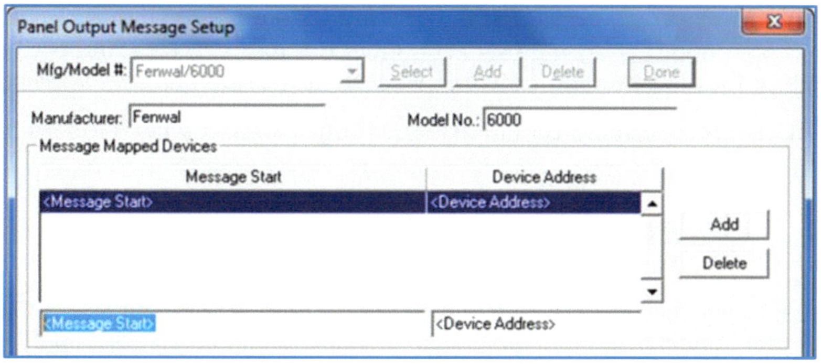

After the pseudo device is automatically created in the database, you will be able to assign a device type, description, and any other information you would like to include in the System Devices list to further clarify the event. You may also want to drop an icon of that device onto your background floor plan – or have it blink on a photograph background picture of the panel on the wall.

Click "Add" to continue adding pseudo points.

Device State Mapping

The bottom half of the Legacy Panel Setup form lists terms as they will be reported from the panel, and assigns them to one of three states: ALARM, TROUBLE or NORMAL.

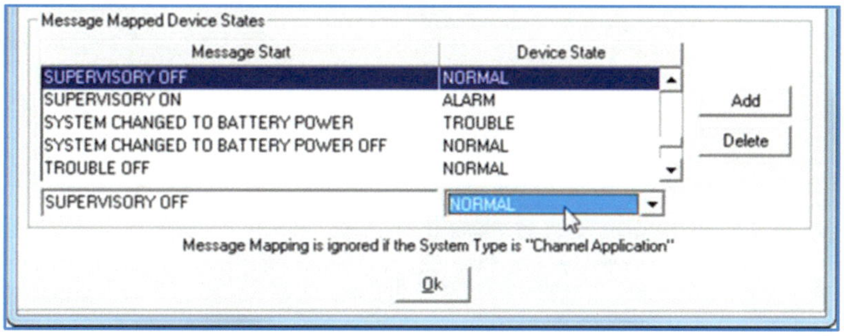

Each item on the left column list will match a message from the control panel. The corresponding choice on the right will determine how the event will behave in System Watch. To change the Device State between the three options, highlight the item in the list, drop down the Device State list to choose between ALARM, TROUBLE, or NORMAL.

You may wonder why there is only one choice for ALARM, and there is no way to distinguish between a FIRE ALARM and a SUPERVISORY ALARM. The type of alarm is determined by the Device Type category. One device type cannot be both a FIRE ALARM and a SUPERVISORY. Use the State/Image menu to modify and determine Logical State for each device type.

Click "Add" to continue adding message mapping for events.

Click "OK" on the bottom of the form when you are through.

Channel Applications

In addition to receiving information from COM ports, RescueLogic can receive information from other Windows programs — in other words, a custom channel application.

A channel application is a Windows program that runs separately from RescueLogic, but is pre-programmed to send messages to RescueLogic and display alarms. A channel number is a RescueLogic convention that allocates numbered pathways for data transfer between RescueLogic and channel applications.

You can use your own in-house programmer and the RescueLogic Software Developers Kit to create new applications.

Using Channel Applications

Channel Applications contain their own interpretation information, and do not use Panel Types information described in the Legacy Panel Types or Script Panel Types sections. To use a Channel Application, just determine which Channel number will be used to report the information. As many as 99 different channels – meaning 99 different Windows applications – can send alarm information to RescueLogic.

To configure your RescueLogic system to read a channel application, start by opening Configuration Manger. Go to the “Setup” drop-down menu and click on “Communication Paths.”

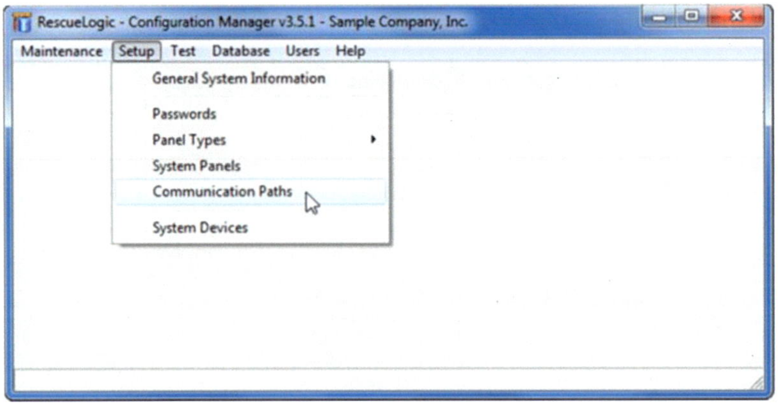

Click the “Add Path” button, or click the port that is already listed.

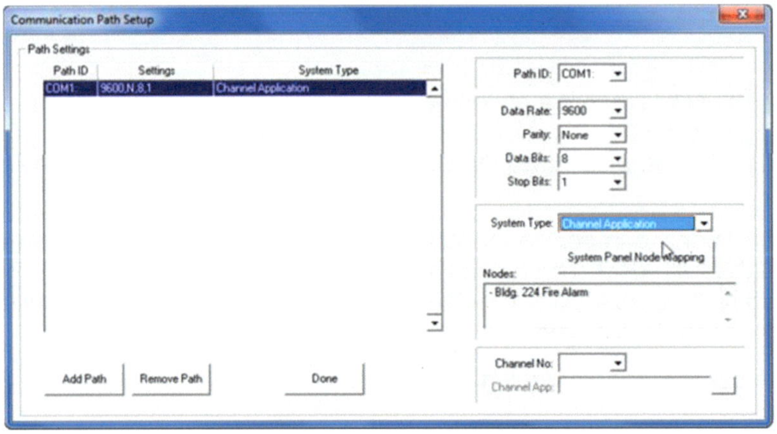

Assign Channel Numbers

On the System Type drop-down list, choose “Channel Application.” Then use the “Channel No” drop-down list to assign a channel number. The number will match a corresponding channel for the other application.

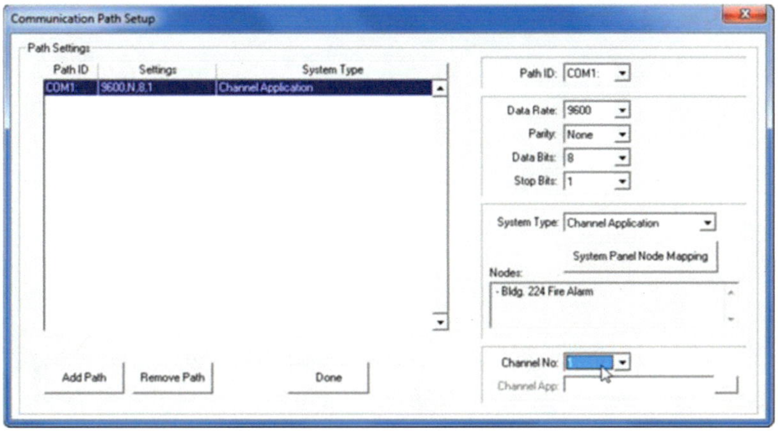

After you have selected your system type and channel number, you must assign each node that will be reported through the channel to a System Panel already defined in the RescueLogic database. Click “System Panel Node Mapping.”

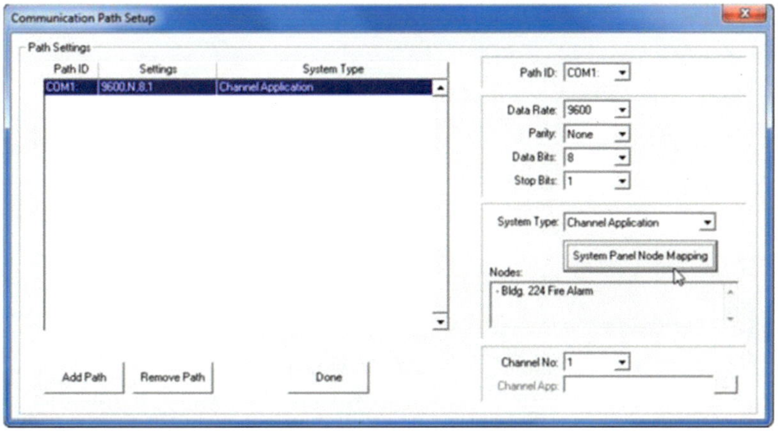

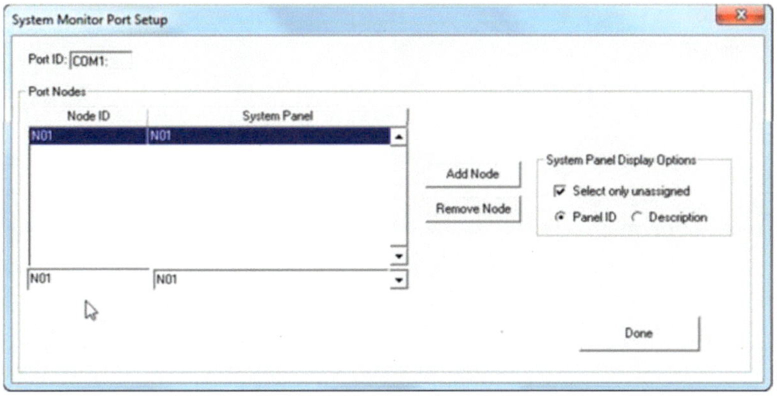

Add all Nodes as they will be reported from your Channel Application, and assign each to a System Panel.

Script Panel Types

Open Configuration Manager and use the “Setup” drop down menu to open “Script Panel Types.”

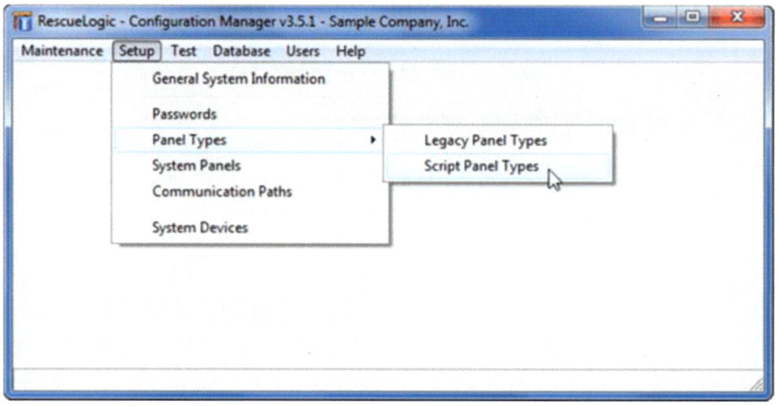

Choose the model of the panel you’re editing, or click “Add” to create a new Panel Type.

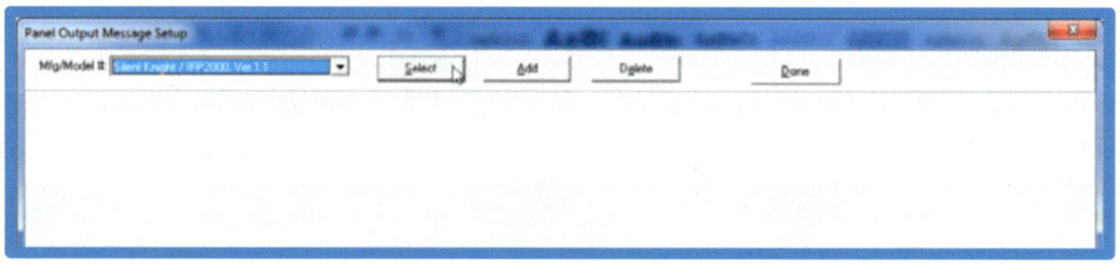

If you added a new Panel Type, enter the manufacturer, model, and version number.

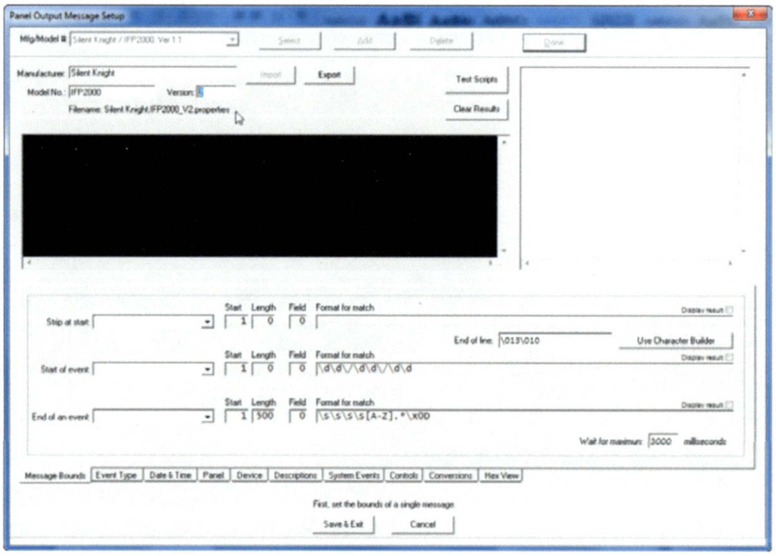

Define Patterns for Data Extraction

Now, look at the tabs on the bottom of the form. Each tab allows you to configure a different aspect of interpreting event messages from your alarm panel. The technique of extracting information will be familiar to many computer programmers. Basically, since the format of messages sent by your fire alarm panel is very consistent, you can define patterns to look for, and extract specific data, like Device Types and Addresses. It's a process that's commonly used by computer programmers. If you'd like to study it further, look for books on regular expression pattern matching, or Regex.

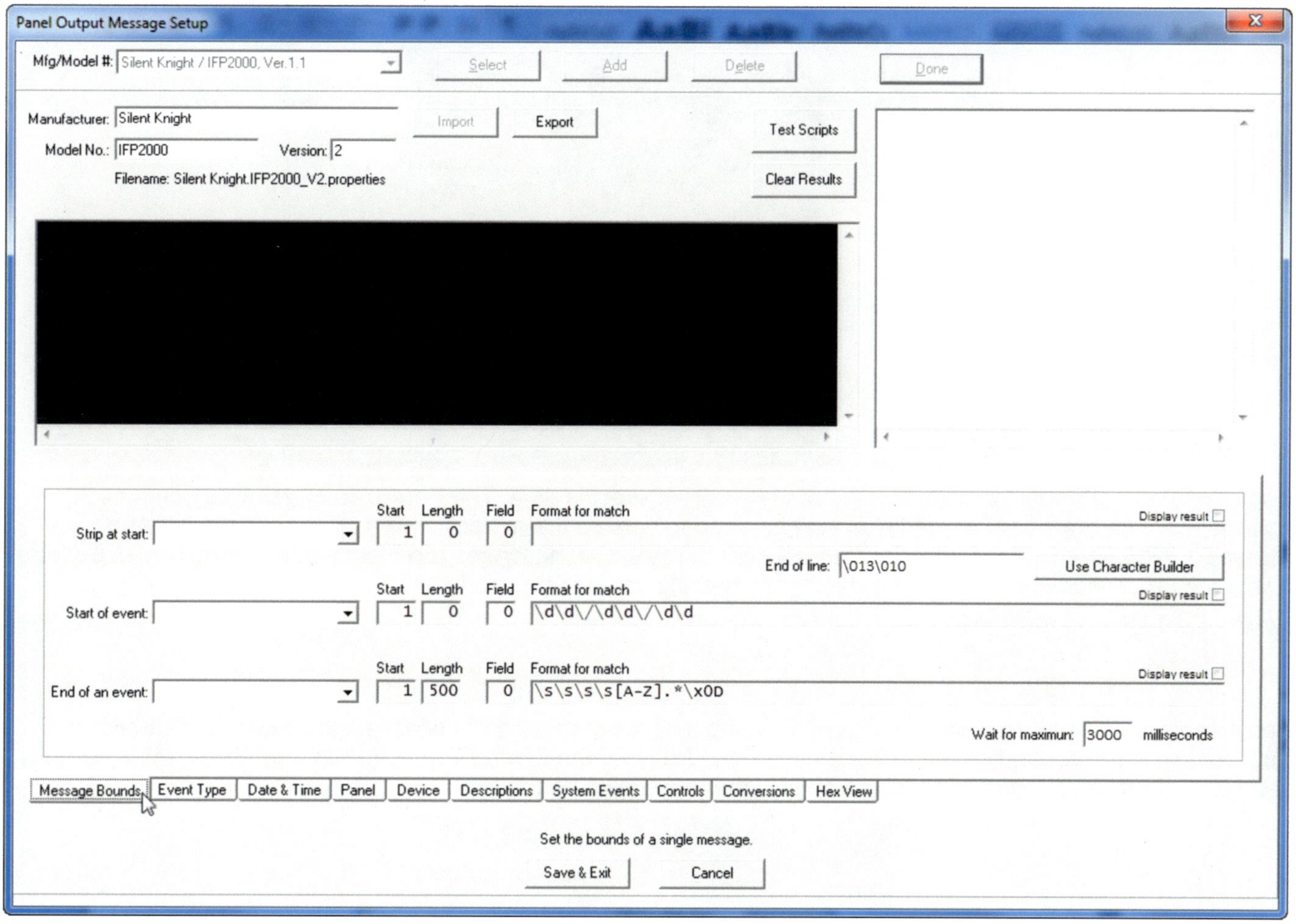

Test Your Scripts

The black box is an area to paste text that was received from alarm panel events, and the white text box shows you the results of your script rules extracting messages from the panel text. Click Test Scripts to see the results of how the patterns are extracted from the sample text pasted in the black box. Click Clear Results to clear the white box between tests.

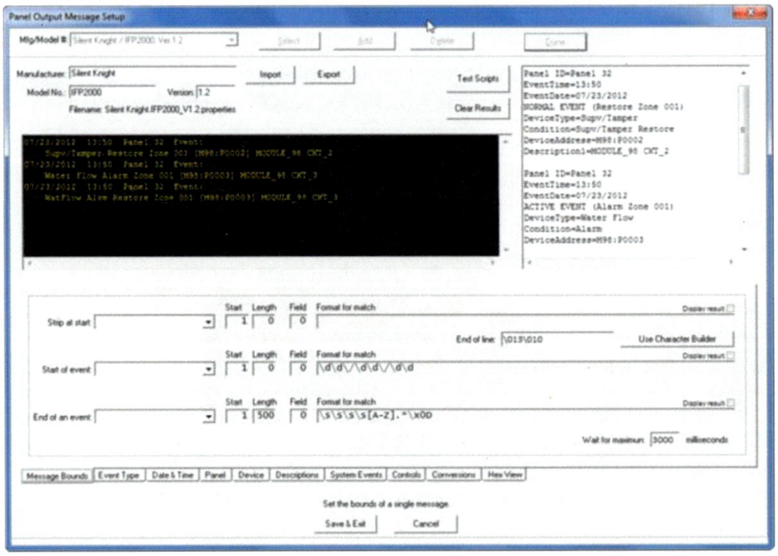

Each Script rule will use the pattern you define to extract specific data. The Format to Match field contains the pattern text. The Start and Length fields may be used to confine the extraction to a specific range within a message. When set to 0, the Length value will search the entire message. The Field value is for complex Scripts. It tells the processor which group of parentheses has the value to be used.

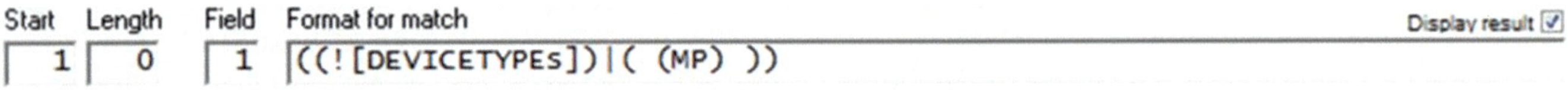

The sample above has an embedded variable name that refers to a list of possible text values. Each Script rule may contain a corresponding list. In this example the list is for the Device Types. In practice, the variable name is replaced with the list of possible text matches in the drop-down on the left.

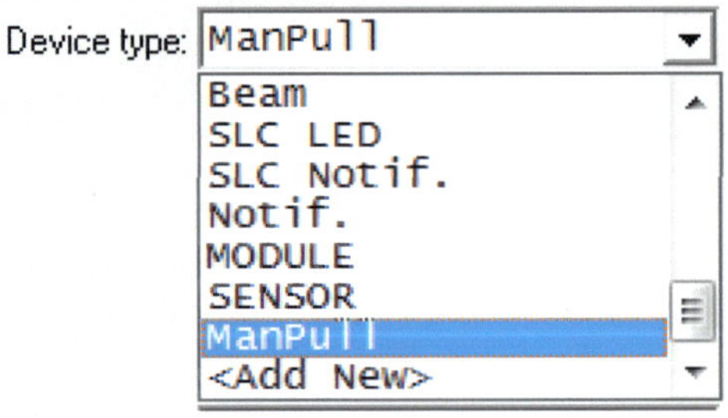

You can check the box below the list to see its Script format, where each item is enclosed in parentheses.

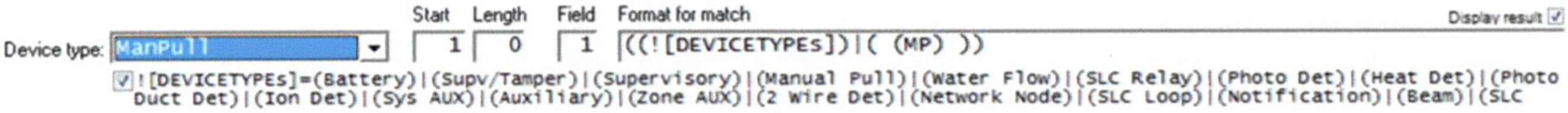

The first tab, Message Bounds, defines the beginning and end of each message. It also allows you to strip specified pattern from the beginning, and set a maximum time to wait for the end of an event.

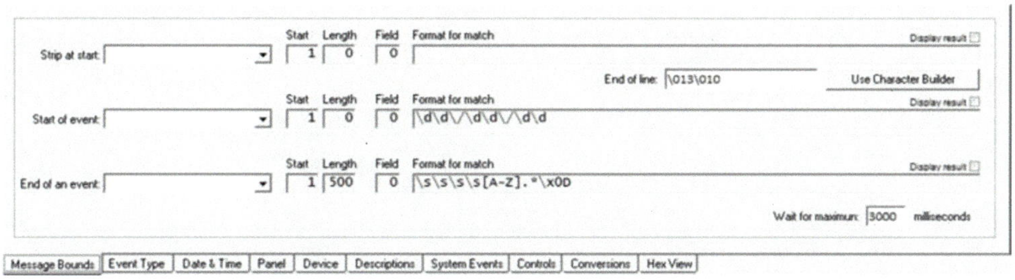

The Event Type tab allows you to define messages that are changes from Alarm, Trouble, and Normal state.

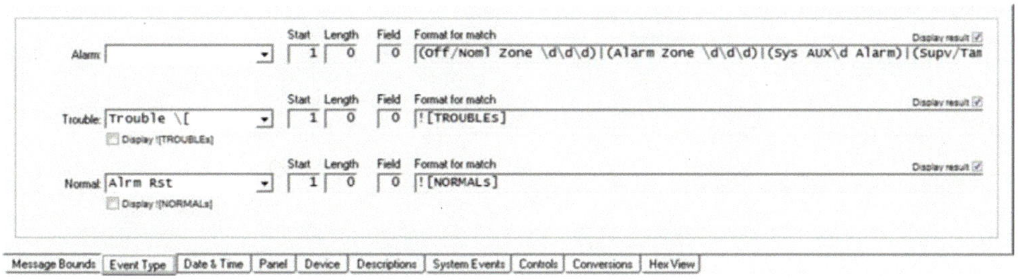

The Date & Time tab defines the format of date and time.

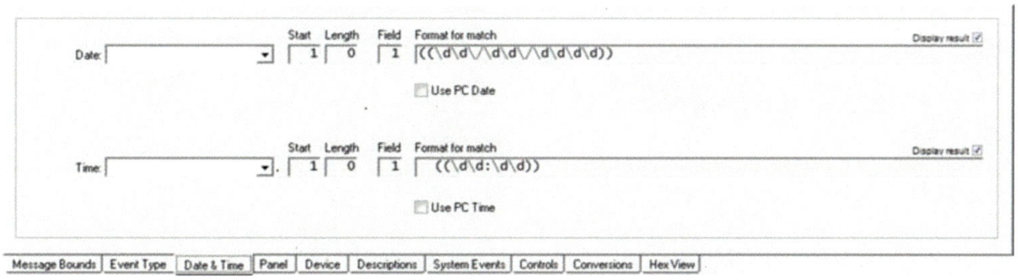

The Panel tab defines Node IDs, panel reset messages, and system events.

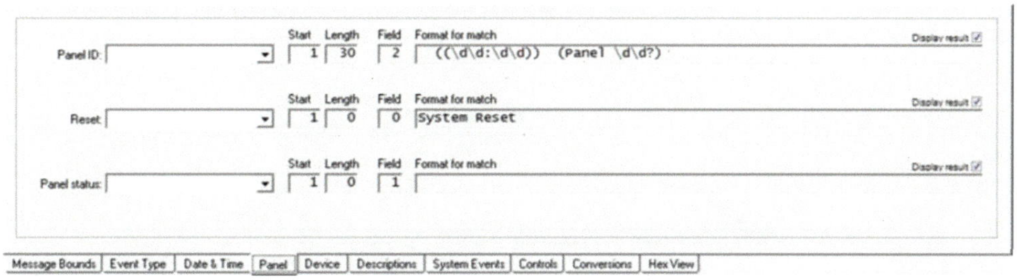

The Device tab allows extraction of Device Type, Address, and Condition text.

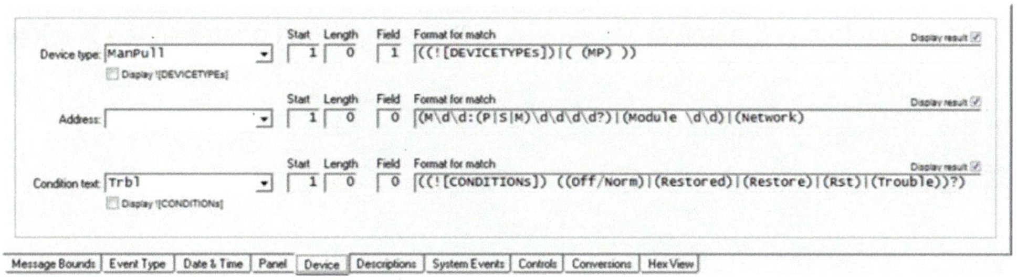

The Description tab allows you to extract Description text from events. If both are found, they are concatenated together to create a single Description for System Watch to display.

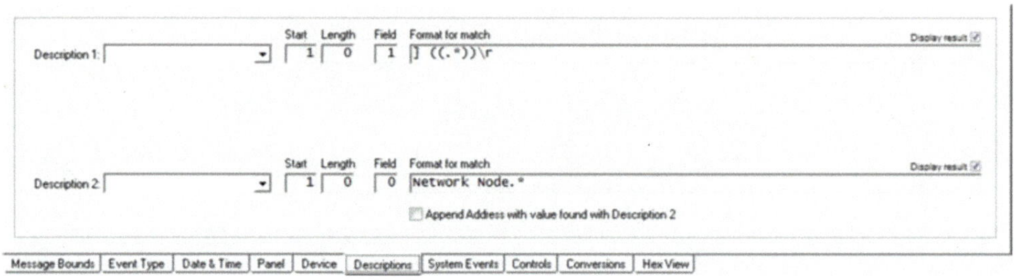

The System Events tab provides the parameters for a Heartbeat, and lets you define messages that are to be completely ignored by RescueLogic.

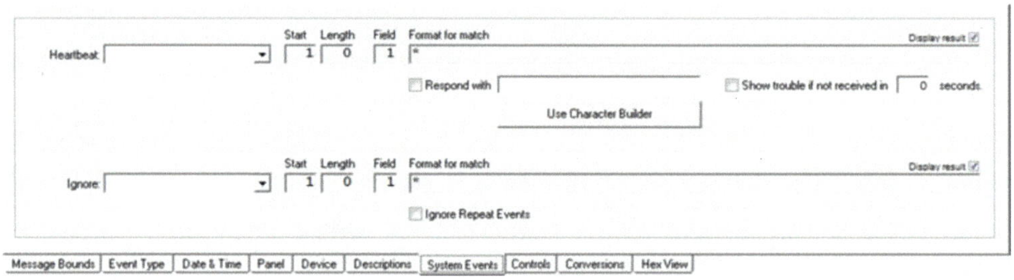

The Controls tab defines pushbuttons for commands to be sent to the panel.

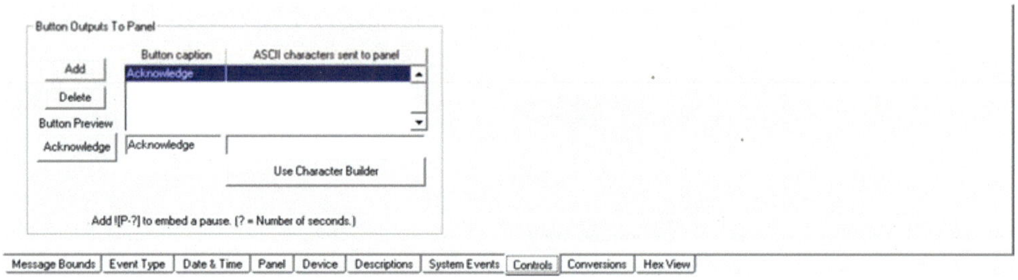

The Conversion tab provides a way to change text as it was extracted, and convert it to something more meaningful for display in System Watch.

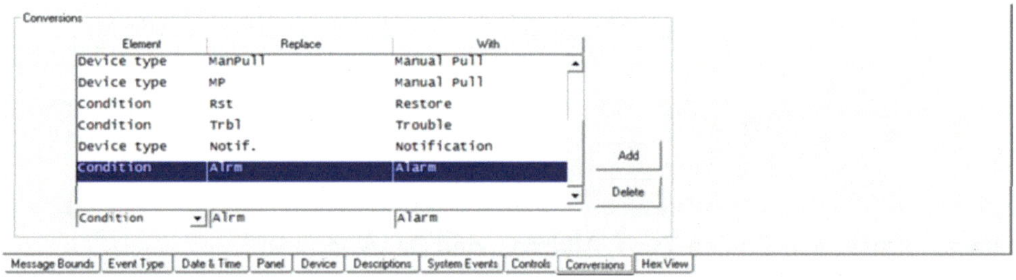

The Hex View tab allows you to see the actual hex values of the sample text pasted in the black window.

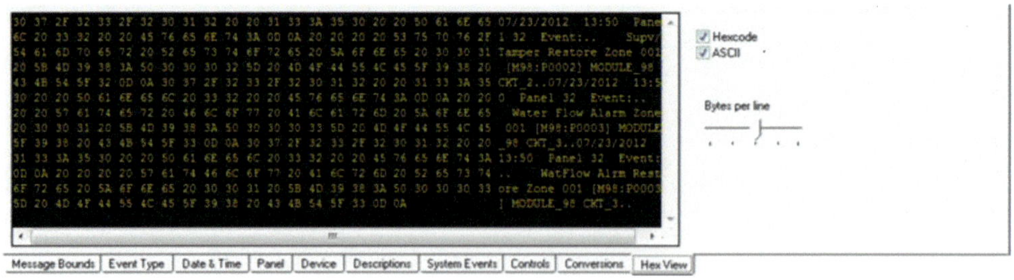

Communication Paths

A communication path is a route for information transfer between a computer and an alarm system. RescueLogic usually relies on two types of communication paths: COM ports and TCP/IP.

A COM port is a plug-in connection. Older technology uses COM ports and RS232 protocol to send information via a modem, a mouse, or a printer. By modern standards, RS232 specifications are slow. They're also limited to 50 feet of standard cable length. (Other protocols, such as RS485, RS422, and fiber optics, can speed up communication and extend the distance between COM port devices.)

Your alarm system probably has an RS232 port on its control panel that you can use to collect data as events occur. In some cases, usually UL-listed systems, information can also go from the computer to the RS232 port.

A TCP/IP connection uses an IP network. It uses the same Ethernet connection that's used for other information transfer, such as Internet access and file sharing between networked computers.

Your fire alarm panel may have an Ethernet port that can plug into an IP network. If your panel has an RS232 or RS485 data port, you can connect it to an IP network with a small device called a serial server.

Many RescueLogic systems use just one communication path — either a COM port or a TCP/IP connection. Those who want to connect several panels and computers, however, combine the two types of connections in order to connect remote COM ports over a local area network.

Configure Your Communication Paths

It's relatively simple to configure communication paths for your RescueLogic system. Start by opening Configuration Manager. Go to the "Setup" drop-down menu and click on "Communication Paths."

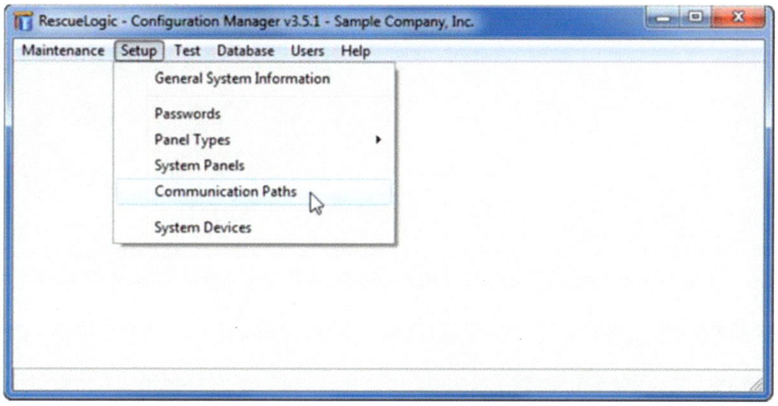

The Communication Path Setup screen will open. You'll notice that RescueLogic comes with a default COM port that's already set up.

Edit Your COM Ports

Click on "COM1." The fields on the right will display the port's parameters: data rate, data bits, parity, and stop bits. You can edit them to match the COM ports you will use.

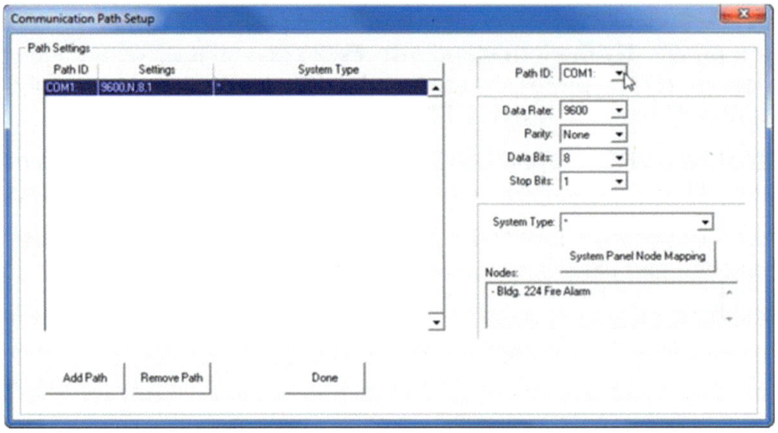

You can use the drop-down Port ID list to select any COM port from 1 to 99.

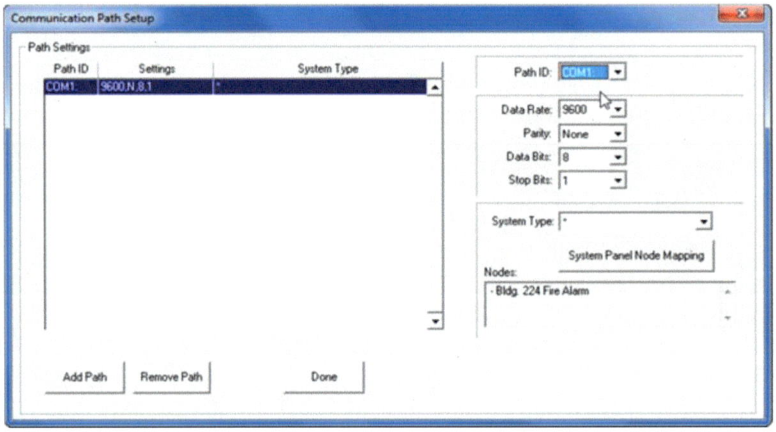

Set the Baud Rate, Parity, Data Bits, and Stop Bits to match the settings of your control panel.

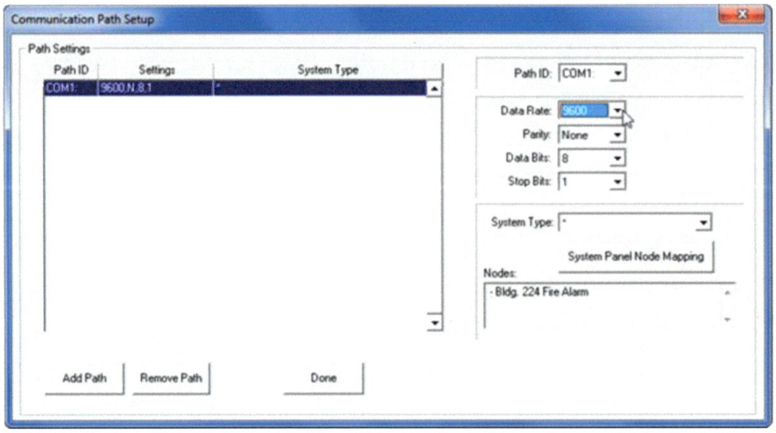

Your system might use TCP/IP connections instead of directly connected RS232 COM ports. In that case, the Baud Rate, Data Bits, and Stop Bits will be set at the remote serial device. If you have a newer panel, it might not use those settings at all. It would simply have an IP Address, and a data Port number. In IP network terms, the IP Address and Port are called a *socket*.

To set the pathway as a direct IP connection, change the Path ID selection to TCP/IP.

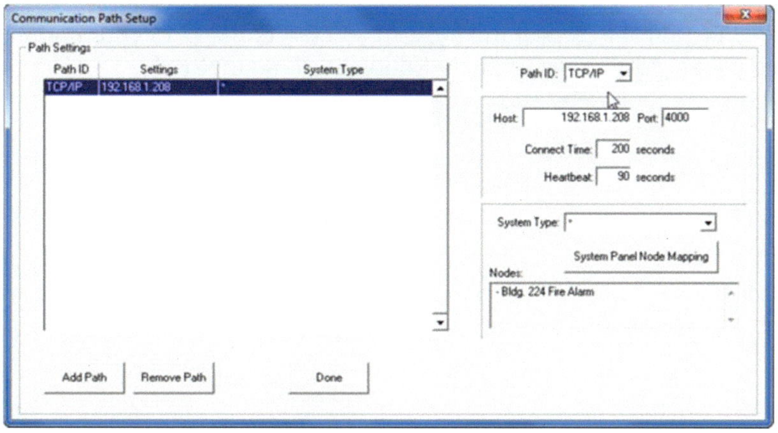

Next, type in the IP Address as the Host, and the data port number as the Port.

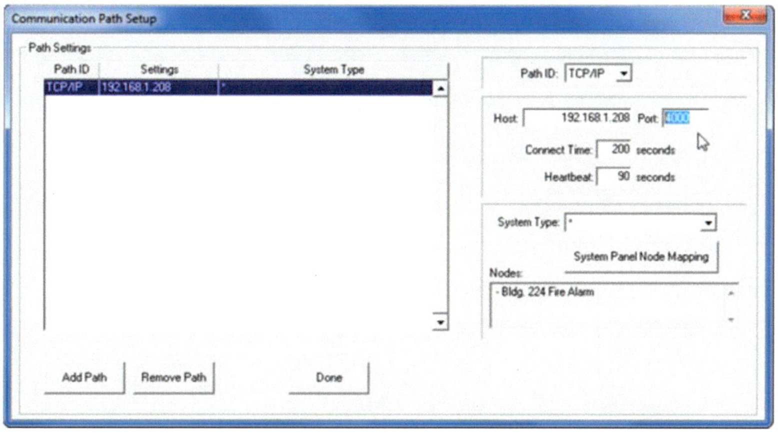

Connect Time is the allowable duration the IP socket may remain disconnected before it will report a problem. NFPA codes require the system to report a problem within 200 seconds. Therefore, the maximum allowable setting for Connect Time is 200. The default Connect Time is 90 seconds.

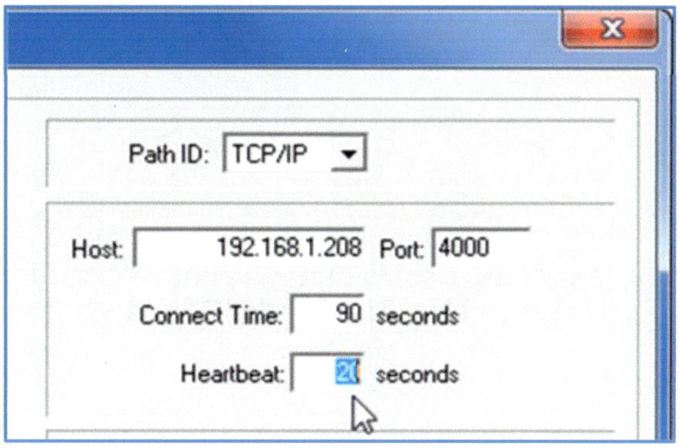

The Heartbeat value is the frequency of sending a string of text to the IP socket as a way to test its connection integrity. This is for systems that do not already have two-way communication. If no data is generated, the IP socket is not tested. For such systems, a heartbeat signal may be generated by RescueLogic as a periodic test of the path. Set the Heartbeat to ‘0’ if your alarm panel is already communicating in both directions through the pathway. The default Heartbeat is 20 seconds.

Use the drop-down “System Type” list to select the system you will connect to your communication path. Select the last item in the list (*) if your system uses the new Script interface method.

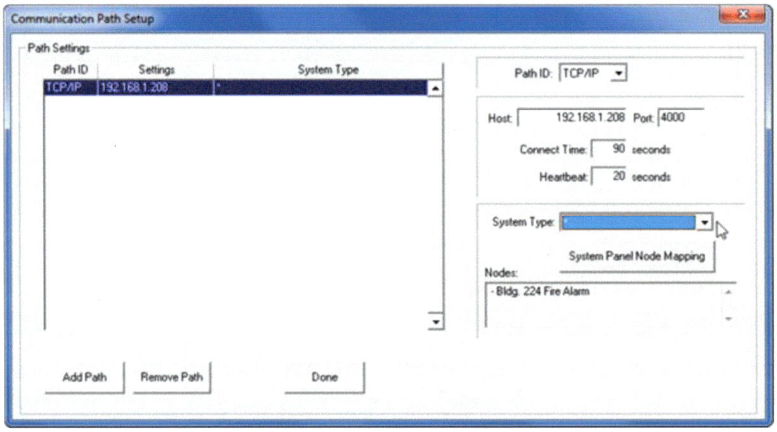

Helpful Hint: Your system might be one of those listed in the “System Type” drop-down list. If your system is not listed, you may use a custom interface, or a field configurable Script interface. Many alarm panel manufacturers have already developed interface solutions for RescueLogic to work with their systems. Call us toll-free at (866) 665-2100 for details, or e-mail info@RescueLogic.net.

Once you have selected your system type, click “System Panel Node Mapping.”

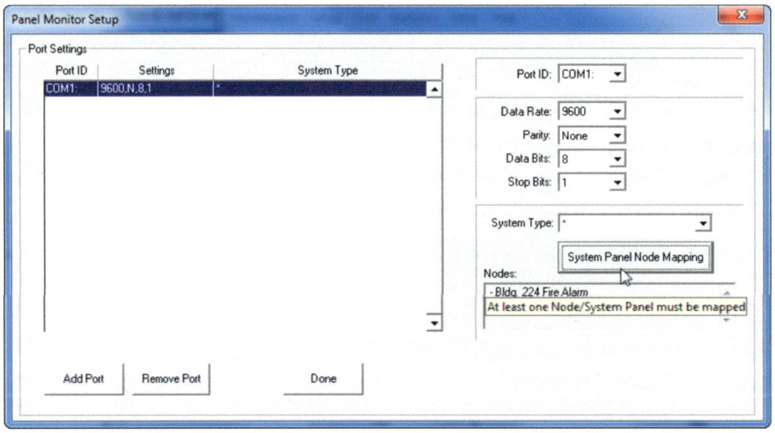

A new setup screen will open, so you can list the panels that will send information through the path. Start by highlighting the default node in the System Panel list. The “Node ID” and “System Panel” name will automatically appear in the fields on the bottom.

Highlight an item in the list. If the window is blank, click “Add Node.”

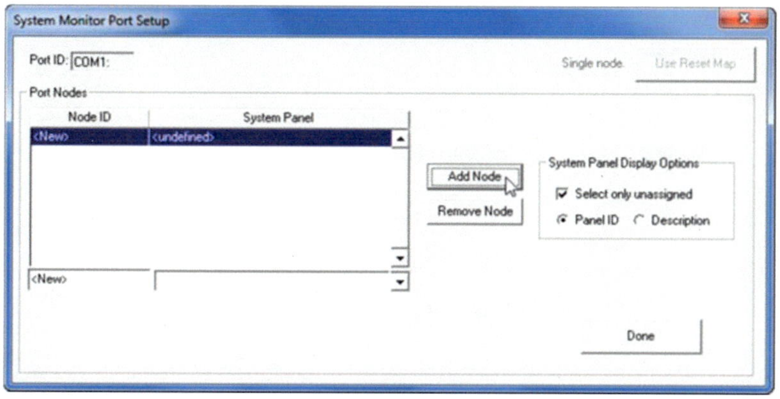

The “Node ID” must match the format that already has been established by your system manufacturer. System Panels defined earlier will appear in the “System Panel” drop-down list.

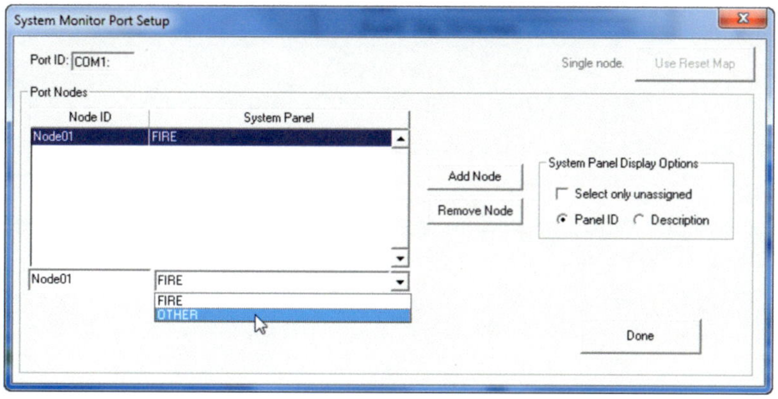

Click the “down” arrow on the System Panel field to see the list of panels you defined earlier using the “Setup System Panels” menu. Select the system panel that will send data to the new port. Repeat as needed for all panels that will report through this path. When you are finished, click “Done.”

The “System Panel” column on this form allows you to see panels listed by either Panel ID or Description as you entered them in your RescueLogic database. You may choose to list panels by either Panel ID or Description. Additionally, if you have a long list of panels, you may want to check “Select only unassigned” to narrow the list as you apply the correct panel to the Node ID you’ve entered.

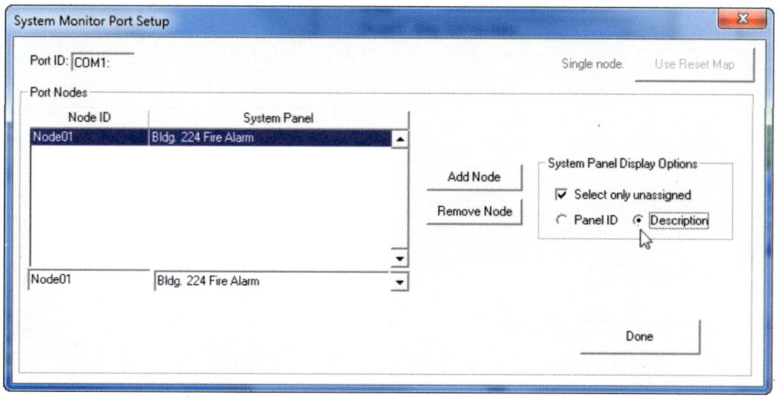

This image shows the same system panels listed by description.

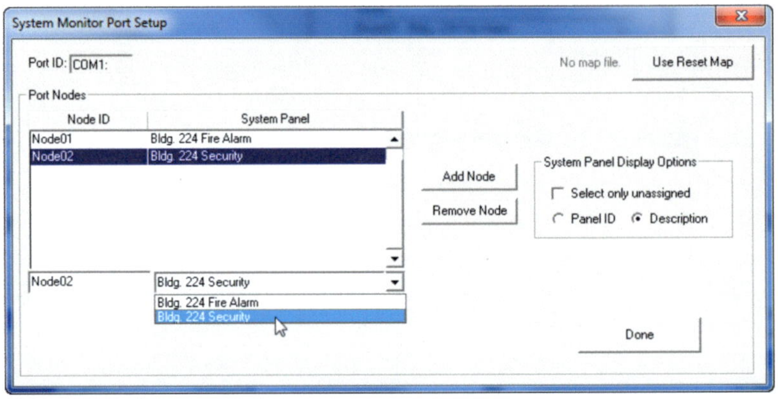

Helpful Hint: Here are some things you'll need to know about nodes:

- If your System Type is not capable of multiple nodes, and allows only one panel, the "Add Node" button may not be usable after you have assigned one system panel. However, the one node and system panel must be assigned to the COM port using this form.
- If the new port receives data and information from more than one source or panel, click "Add Node." You will see "<New>" added to the list. Change the text to an appropriate entry, such as "Node02."
- Enter ID exactly as it will be reported by each panel as a Node ID. The network message will tell RescueLogic which panel is reporting.

Add a Reset Map

Some multi-node alarm systems allow a reset action on one panel to reset other nodes as well. The system may not report that other panels have been reset, and all devices are cleared. In order for RescueLogic to correctly represent those devices, you'll need to add a Reset Map.

Click the button on the upper right labeled Reset Map.

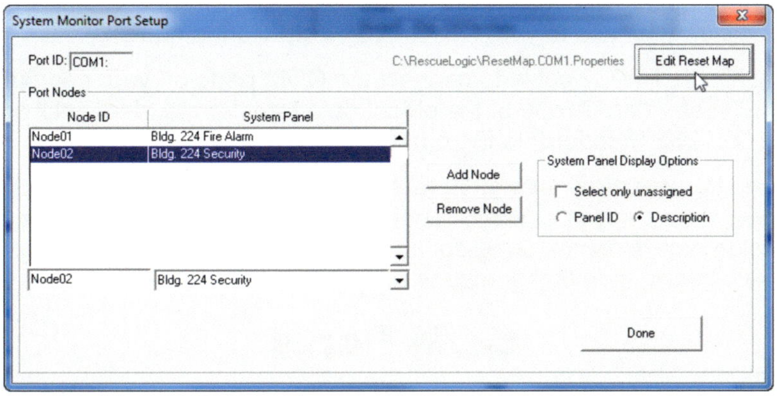

A new screen will appear that allows you to create statements about any nodes that reset other nodes (but do not report the event.) In this example, the statement means that a reset message about Node01 also performed a reset at Node02.

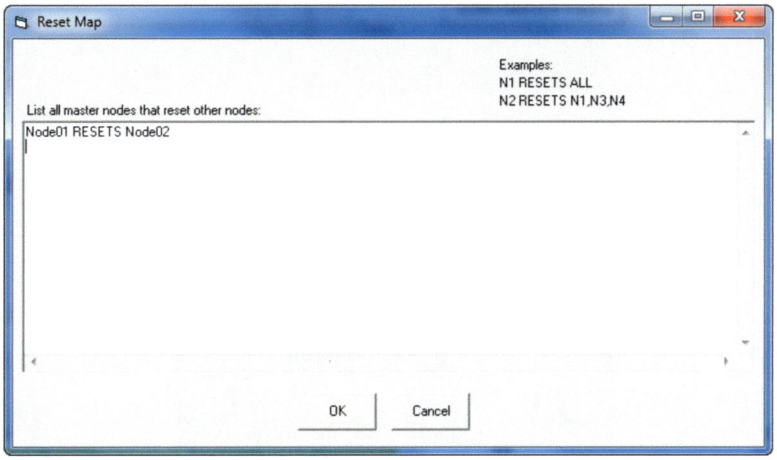

Click "OK" to go back to the Panel Monitor Setup screen. Double-check your port assignments and panel types, make corrections as needed, and then click "Done" to return to the Configuration Manager main screen.

Serial Connections

Up until this point, you have been configuring RescueLogic software for the big moment when you actually connect your alarm panels to the COM ports on your RescueLogic computer. We have worked with hundreds of RescueLogic installations, and we are happy to give you our advice about the hardware and peripherals you will use to link ports and panels.

You can use practically any combination of cabling, network switches, and wireless networking devices to connect all of the devices from panels on your site to your RescueLogic monitoring station.

You may use commonly available RS232 cable to connect the COM ports on your computer to the COM ports on your alarm panel. (The RS232 standard is one of the oldest data transfer standards still applicable to computers today. It was renamed the "EIA232 Standard" in the early 1990's.)

An RS232 cable is designed to run a maximum of 50 feet. In its most basic form, it's twisted pair copper wire, consisting of a common wire, a transmit wire, and a receive wire. The three wires work together to complete an electrical circuit. The common wire is continuously connected. The transmit wire pulses to transmit a code. And the receive wire receives any information that comes in from the transmit wire of another device.

COM Ports

COM ports, also known as serial ports, are one of the most basic ways to get data into and out of a computer. COM ports are the "plug ins" that, in earlier times, let you attach devices, like modems and printers, to your computer. When you set up your RescueLogic system, you will use COM ports to attach your system panels to your RescueLogic computer. COM ports are usually nine-pin ports that look like this:

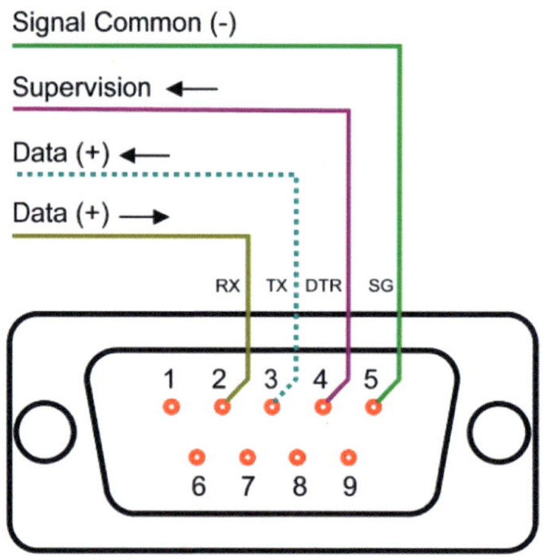

CADgraphics PC
EIA232 Port
COM1 or COM2

Most desktop computers still come with one COM port. If you need more ports to handle the panels on your site — or to connect to your printer or other peripherals — you can add them quickly and easily:

If you need to add one or two COM ports to your computer, you can plug an adaptor cable into any available USB port.

By combining TCP/IP networks with COM ports, you can add thousands of panels to your RescueLogic system.

COM Port to COM Port Connections

This diagram illustrates a COM port to COM port connection in its simplest form. Technically speaking, you only need two wires to connect your RescueLogic COM port to an alarm panel's COM port: a common wire and a transmit wire running from a panel's transmit pin to the RescueLogic receive pin. In theory, you can also connect the RescueLogic transmit pin to the alarm panel's receive pin. If your RescueLogic system is UL listed, you could transmit information from RescueLogic to the alarm panel, to control the alarms. In practice, you might actually want to double check that RescueLogic does not transmit information to the alarm panel, to ensure that your RescueLogic station is used strictly for monitoring purposes.

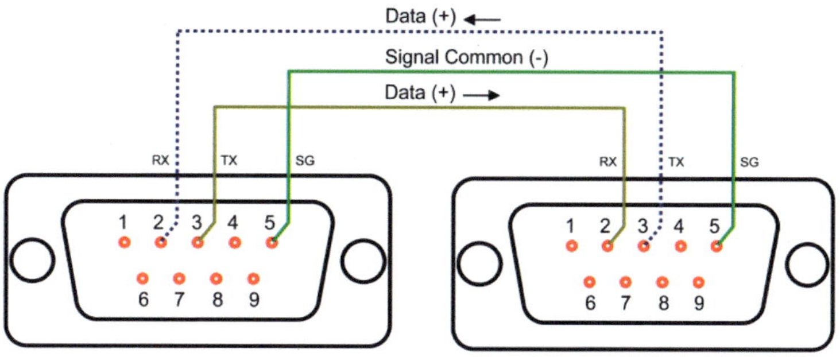

Here is a sample diagram that shows the COM port connector on a fire alarm panel, wired to the COM port on a computer.

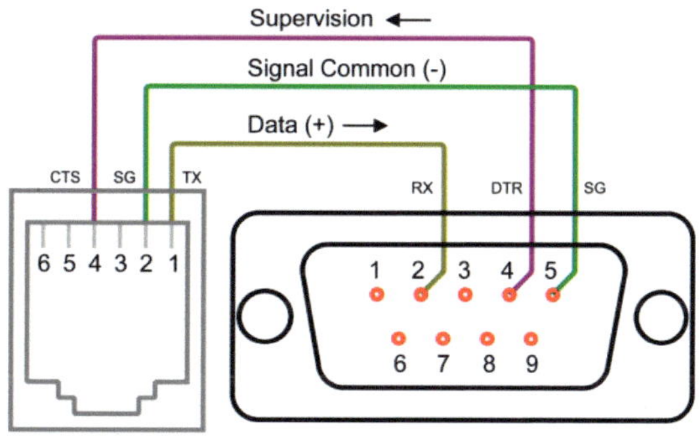

Helpful Hint: If you need to connect your RescueLogic computer to a panel that is more than 50 feet away, you can use converters that will carry the signal over twisted pair copper wire, fiber optic cable, or a wireless signal. The best method is a serial-to-IP converter. Having an IP address makes it possible for RescueLogic to supervise the IP address and report when it is powered down or disconnected.

Ethernet Connections: Add a MOXA Device

A MOXA Device — an NPort serial device server — makes it easy to connect your alarm panels to an Ethernet network so you can monitor them with RescueLogic® software.

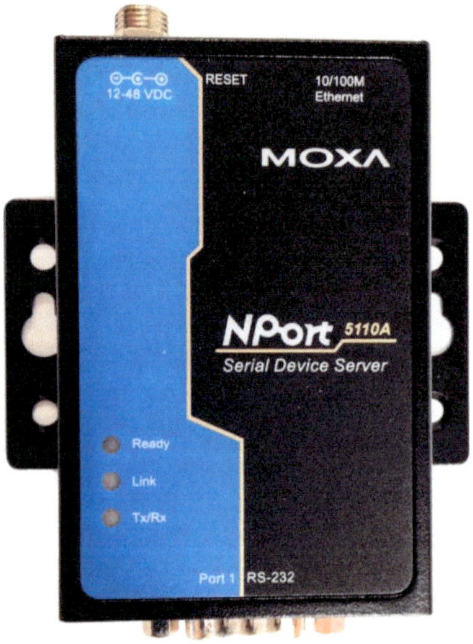

To begin, insert the CD or download the install program from the web. Then run the NPort Search Utility from your Windows menu.

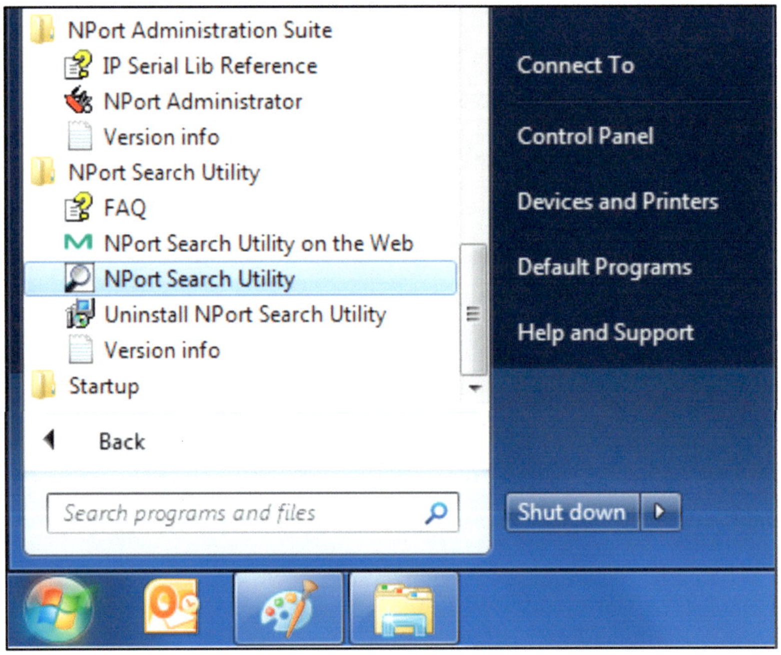

The Search Utility will open. Click the “Search” button to continue.

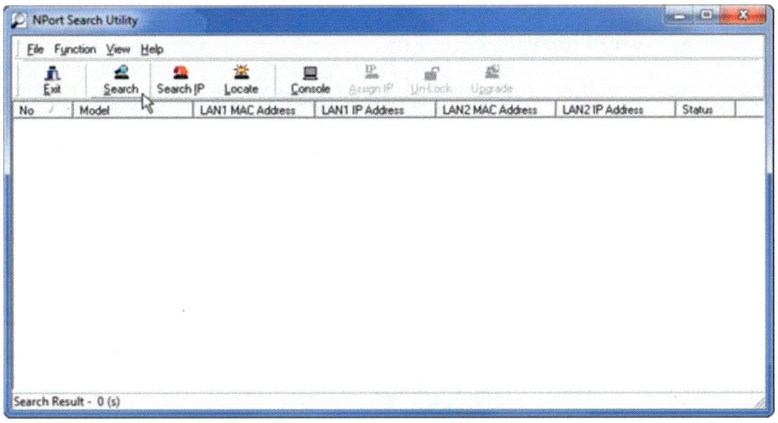

Helpful Hint: The default IP address of a MOXA NPort is 192.168.127.254. If you set your LAN card configuration settings with an IP address in the same subnet (such as 192.168.127.100), you do not necessarily need the Search Utility software. Just skip to the web configuration shown on page 28, and type 192.168.127.254 in the Address bar of your browser.

A new popup window titled “Searching” will appear for several seconds, list any MOXA NPorts, then disappear.

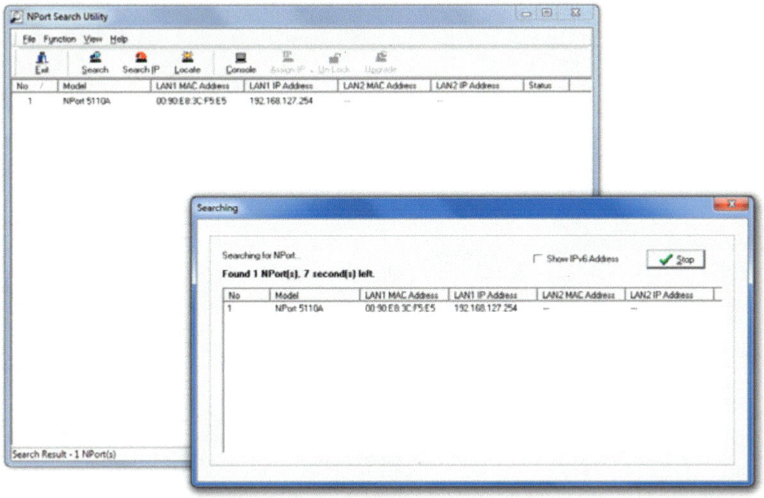

After the search window disappears, the list on the list window should show the NPort server with the default IP Address 192.168.127.254. Double-click the list item to open a browser window and configure.

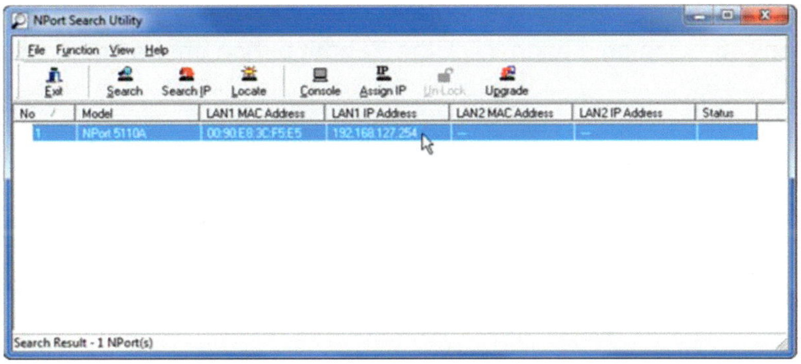

The NPort configuration screen will appear in a web browser. The IP Address of the server will show in your browser's address bar. The left column has a menu for changing settings. You will need to use three of them: Operating Settings, Serial Settings, and Network Settings.

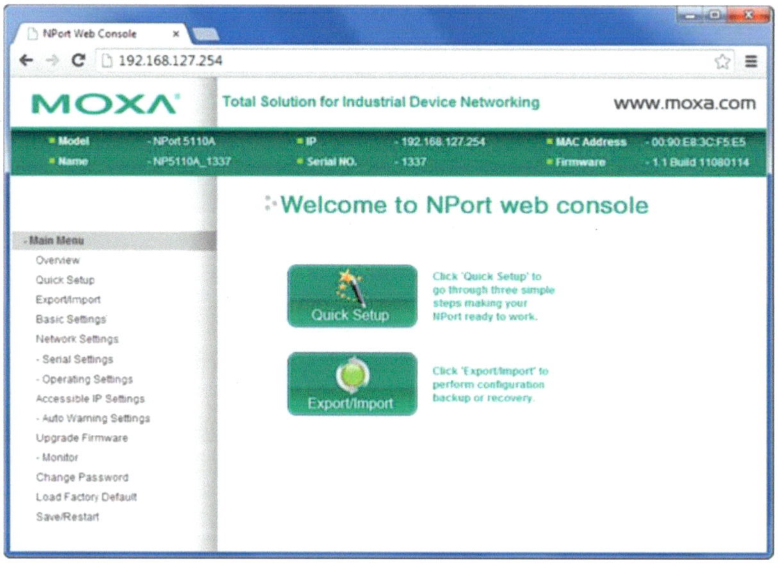

If you like, you can also change the name of the server from the Basic Settings menu.

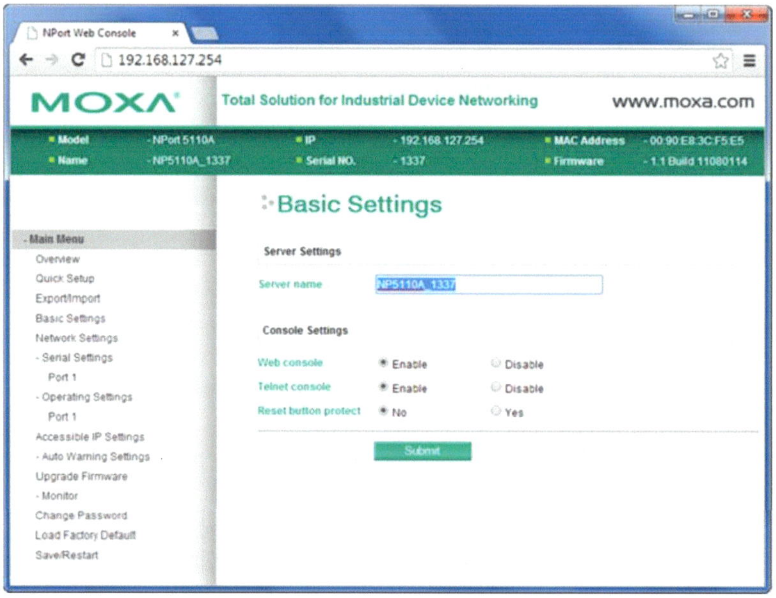

When you are done with any changes on a page, click the Submit button on the bottom of the page.

Configure Operating Settings

From the Main Menu in the left-hand column, click "Port 1" under the Operating Settings label.

Change the default "RealCOM" operation mode to "TCP Server." This setting allows the IP Address socket to be supervised by RescueLogic, rather than simulate a COM Port.

Change TCP alive check time from "7" to "0." This allows RescueLogic to reconnect immediately when System Monitor is restarted. The default 7 minutes would make the server wait that long before a reconnect.

Change Max connection from "1" to "4" to allow connections from remote computers for testing.

Note the default "4001" setting for "Local TCP Port." The IP Address and this port number are the values that you will enter in RescueLogic for the socket connection.

Click "Submit."

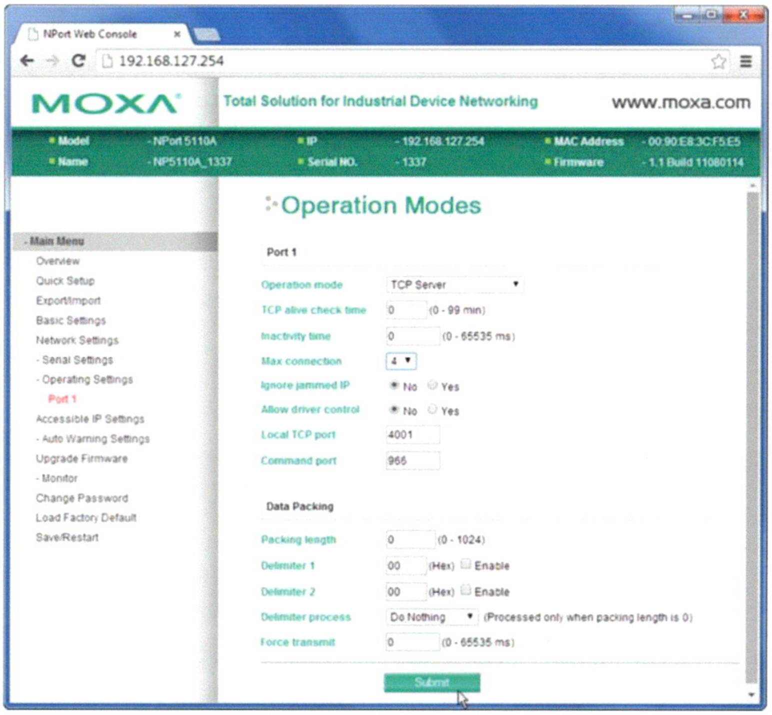

Now click "Save/Restart."

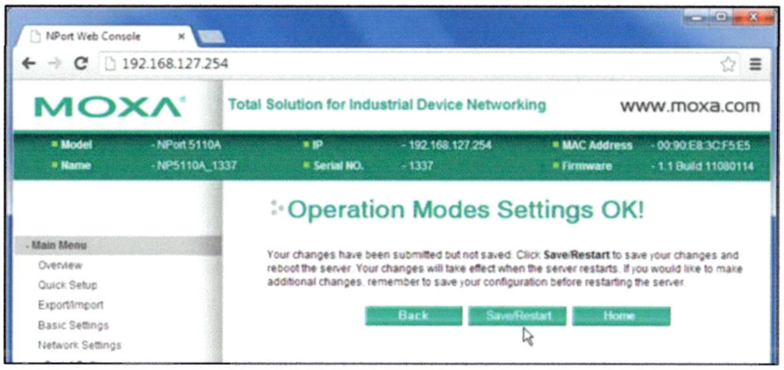

Configure Serial Settings

The serial settings of the NPort must match the alarm panel or printer interface module that you will connect to.

Click "Port 1" on the left menu column, under Serial Settings. Set the baud rate, data bits, stop bits, and parity to match the values specified in the alarm system manufacturer's instructions.

Click "Submit."

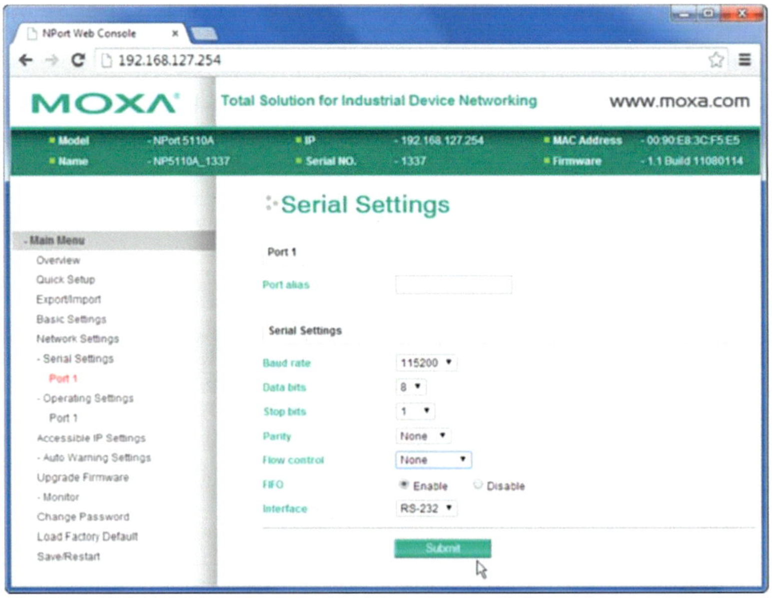

On the page that appears, click "Save/Restart."

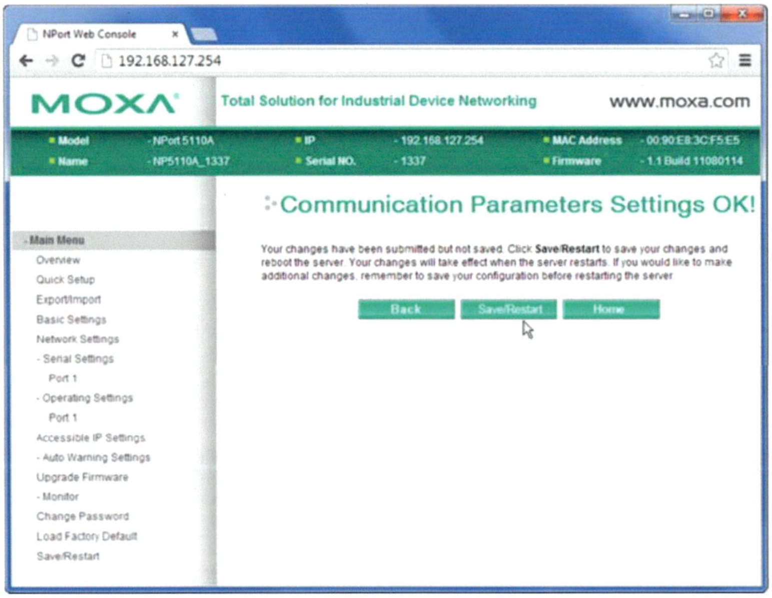

Configure Network Settings

Click "Network Settings," under the "Main Menu" in the left-hand column. The network administrator should have provided a static IP Address for use with each serial server. Fill in the blanks to match your system's information: change the IP Address, Gateway, Netmask and DNS Servers. Leave IP configuration set with the default value "Static."

The SNMP settings are not used, so you can leave the factory defaults

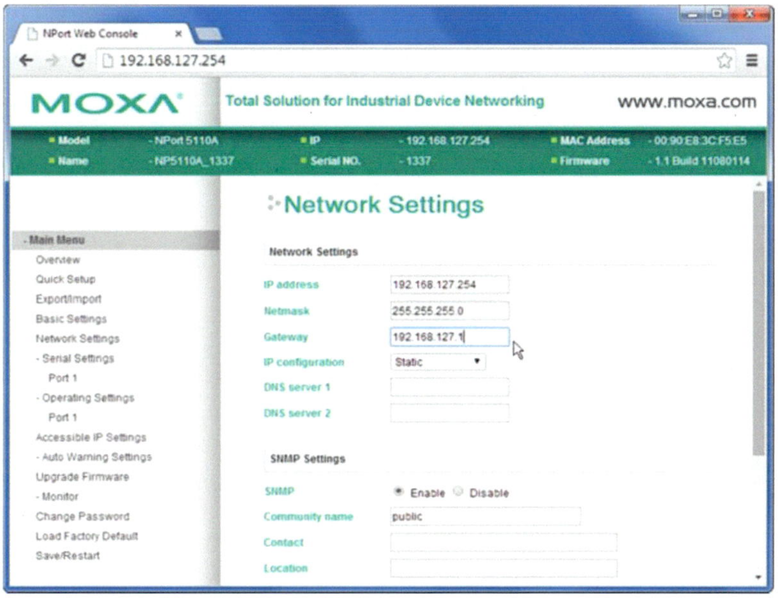

Scroll to the bottom and click "Submit."

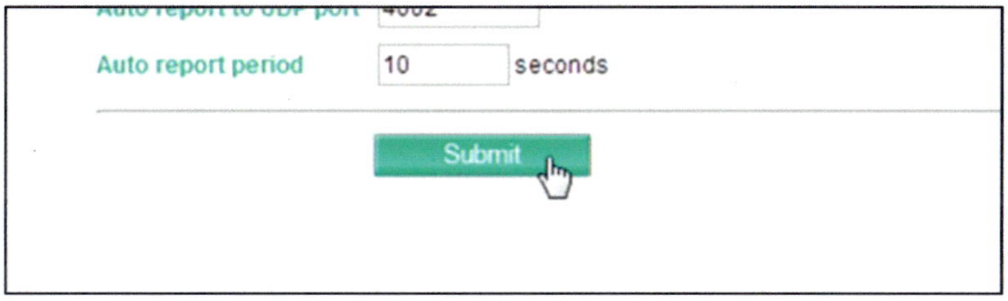

Another page appears to confirm that you are ready to make the changes permanent. Click "Save/Restart."

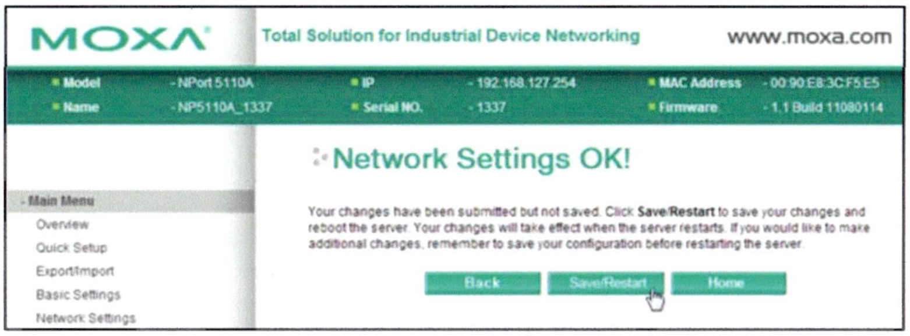

The IP Address is now changed, and your browser must be changed to match.

When you click on a link, you might see a page with a message that the page failed to load.

Type the changed address in your browser's Address bar and Refresh to see the MOXA configuration page again.

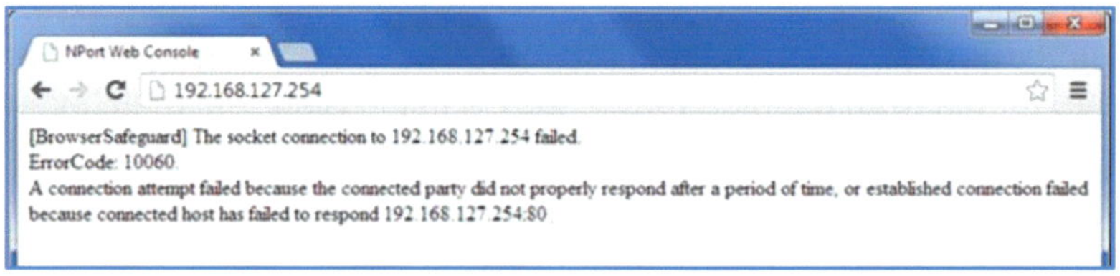

Your serial server is now ready to communicate with RescueLogic. See RescueLogic's *Complete Guide* for the next steps.

Helpful Hint: If your browser does not find the server with the default or the newly assigned IP Address, check the IP settings of your computer's network adapter. The left three quad elements of the IP Address represent the network, and the right quad element is unique for each endpoint device. Remember to write down your computer's original settings first. Contact your network administrator if these settings are not familiar to you.

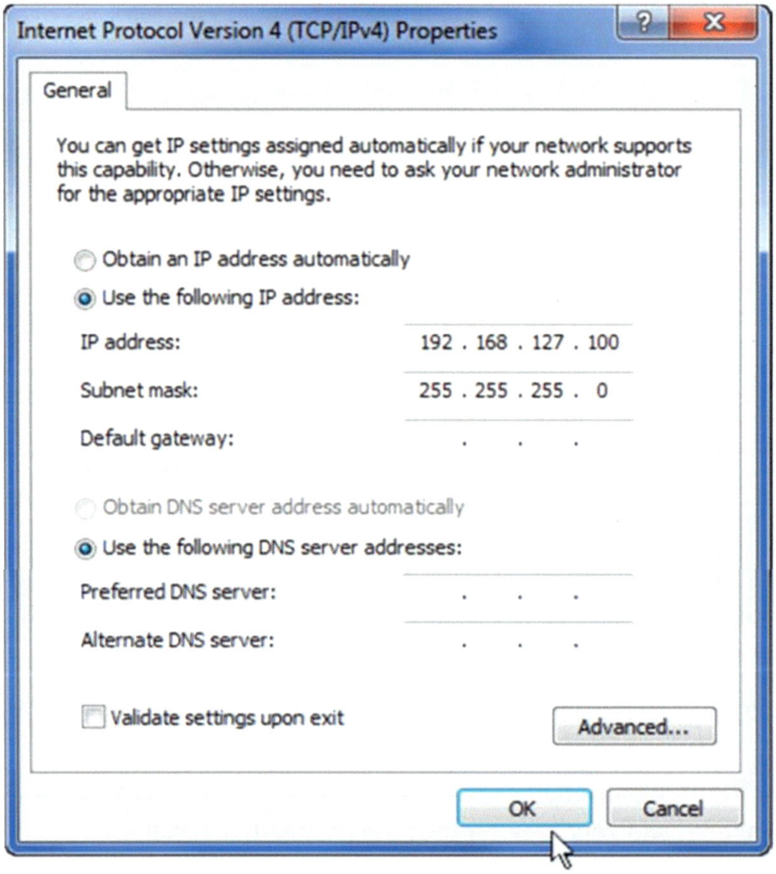

Questions or Comments?

Technical support is available online at RescueLogic.com, or by phone at (612) 722-3233.

Get the Complete Guide to RescueLogic Software

Get the most from your RescueLogic software, with comprehensive instructions and step-by-step illustrations.
Download a PDF copy from RescueLogic.com or order a printed book from Amazon.com.

Get more RescueLogic guides at RescueLogic.com

The System Watch handbook introduces RescueLogic to the users who need it most: your site's security guards, emergency dispatchers, and first responders.

In an emergency, you need to communicate clearly with your safety and security team. If they speak Spanish, your RescueLogic system should, too.

Add audible alerts to your RescueLogic System. It's easy to customize your own emergency messages, so everyone knows what's going on.

Copyright Information

Patent Information

Cadgraphics and RescueLogic techniques and technology are protected by United States Patents 6,229,429 and 6,369,695.

Trademark Information

Cadgraphics and RescueLogic are registered trademarks of Cadgraphics Incorporated. "Safety Made Simple" is the service mark of Cadgraphics Incorporated.

Disclaimer

Although every precaution has been taken in the preparation of this guide, the author and the publisher assume no responsibility for errors or omissions. The information in this guide is subject to change without notice to improve reliability, design, and function. This guide does not represent a commitment or a contract on behalf of Cadgraphics Incorporated. In no event will Cadgraphics Incorporated, its agents, or its representatives be liable for direct, indirect, special, incidental, or consequential damages arising out of the use or inability to use the product or documentation, even if advised of the possibility of such damages. The entire risk as to the results and performance of Cadgraphics' RescueLogic software is assumed by you.

Made in United States
Troutdale, OR
11/03/2026

56844684R00024